LUDW

MW00770382

LETTERS
TO C. K. OGDEN

with Comments on
the English Translation
of the
Tractatus Logico-Philosophicus

LUDWIG WITTGENSTEIN

LETTERS
TO C. K. OGDEN

with Comments on
the English Translation
of the
Tractatus Logico-Philosophicus

Edited with an Introduction by
G. H. von WRIGHT

and an Appendix of Letters by
FRANK PLUMPTON RAMSEY

Basil Blackwell, Oxford
Routledge & Kegan Paul, London and Boston

First published in 1973
by Basil Blackwell, Oxford
and
Routledge & Kegan Paul Ltd
Broadway House, 68–74 Carter Lane,
London EC4V 5EL and
9 Park Street, Boston, Mass. 02108, U.S.A.

Printed in Great Britain by
William Clowes & Sons, Limited, London, Beccles and Colchester
and bound by Kemp Hall Bindery, Oxford

First published as a
paperback in 1983
ISBN 0 7100 9482 5

CONTENTS

FOREWORD

THE late C. K. Ogden preserved material of great interest relating to the publication in England of Wittgenstein's famous logico-philosophical treatise, the *Tractatus*. The material consists of the following main items:

1. A copy (off-print), with extensive corrections by Wittgenstein himself, of the printing of his "Logisch-philosophische Abhandlung" in Ostwald's *Annalen der Naturphilosophie* for 1921. It was evidently from this (corrected) off-print that the German text of the book was printed in England in 1922.

2. A typescript of the translation into English of Wittgenstein's work. The translation was probably made from an off-print of the publication by Ostwald, and not from Wittgenstein's own typescript of the German text. The typescript of the translation has numerous changes and corrections in ink by Ogden and by Wittgenstein and some, it seems, by Russell.

3. Fourteen letters from Wittgenstein to Ogden. To two of the letters are attached, on separate sheets, extensive comments referring to points in the English translation.

4. A typed Questionnaire, prepared by Ogden, relating to the translation. The questionnaire is heavily annotated in Ogden's and Wittgenstein's hands.

5. A set of page proofs of the German–English parallel text of the *Tractatus* with annotations and corrections by Ogden and by Wittgenstein and occasionally, it seems, also by F. P. Ramsey. The set does not include proofs of Russell's Introduction.

6. A number of letters and other communications from Ramsey, Russell, and Ostwald to Ogden of 1921–1924, and a few letters of a later date, relating to the translation and publication history of the *Tractatus*.

Published here are the letters and comments mentioned under

3, a facsimile of the Questionnaire (4), and selections from letters mentioned under 6. An Appendix contains some letters from Ramsey to Wittgenstein and additional material which illuminates the relations between the two men. The Ramsey material is published by kind permission of Mrs Lettice Ramsey.

The letters and comments by Wittgenstein make constant reference to the text which was printed by Ostwald, to the typescript of the English translation, and to the page-proofs of the parallel-text. In order to understand these references comparison with the sources is necessary. Since the sources are not reproduced here, the Editor has had to provide comments. A main objective of these comments is to enable the reader to compare the original form of the translation with the version finally printed and to note the transformations between these two extreme stages.

Wittgenstein's English, particularly the orthography, was not too good at the time when he corresponded with Ogden about the publication of his book in England. It is important that the reader should realize this. The Editor has not interfered with grammar or idiom. When Wittgenstein's spelling of English words omits letters, these have been added in square brackets. Letters wrongly added by Wittgenstein have been enclosed in angular brackets. Faulty spelling which cannot be put right by means of either of these two devices, has been corrected without comment. Occasionally, the Editor has also interfered with the punctuation, *e.g.* in some places where the omission of commas or question-marks makes it difficult to understand the meaning of a context.

The Editor has, on the whole, refrained from comments of an evaluating character. Any reader interested in Wittgenstein's *Tractatus* will easily see that the material here published throws valuable light on the original English translation of the book, and occasionally also on Wittgenstein's thoughts themselves. The material further establishes the unqualified truth of C. K. Ogden's words in his prefatory note to the English edition that "the proofs of the translation and the version of the original which appeared in the final number of Ostwald's *Annalen der Naturphilosophie* (1921) have been very carefully revised by the author himself". It is unfortunate that the veracity of this statement became a matter of dispute—now happily ended.

My Introduction contains a brief account of the most important events relating to the translation and publication of Wittgenstein's book in England. A more detailed and extended account of the origin and publication of the *Tractatus* is given in my introductory essay to the publication (1971) by Routledge and Kegan Paul of the early version of the book called the "Prototractatus". At the time when the longer essay was written, some of the facts mentioned in this Introduction were not yet accessible or known to me. The present Introduction therefore in some respects supplements and, on a few points of minor detail, corrects the earlier historical account.

In working out my textual comments and when checking Wittgenstein's references to the typescript (2) and the proofs (5), I have relied on the unfailing and generous assistance of Mr Mark Haymon. I am indebted to Mr Kenneth Blackwell, Director of the Bertrand Russell Archives at McMaster University, Hamilton, Ontario, for copies of the relevant items in the correspondence between C. K. Ogden and Bertrand Russell and for valuable comments on my draft of an Introduction. The letters from Russell are here reproduced with the kind permission of the Editorial Committee of the Archives. My thanks are due to Dr H. Hänsel for copies of F. P. Ramsey's letters to Wittgenstein and to Mrs Lettice Ramsey for permission to publish them. Finally, I wish to thank Mr T. Nyberg for his help with the preparation of the text and the comments for publication.

Helsinki,   GEORG HENRIK VON WRIGHT
March 1971

INTRODUCTION

WITTGENSTEIN finished his "Logisch-philosophische Abhandlung" in the summer of 1918 when he was on a longish leave from
the army. Before returning to the Austro-Italian front he took
steps to find a publisher for his book. After the surrender of the
Austrian army in November 1918 he was a prisoner of war in
Italy until August of the following year. Immediately after his
return he resumed his efforts to get the work published in
Austria or Germany. He approached five different publishers in
all, but without success, notwithstanding the assistance of
Bertrand Russell. In July 1920, when the German publisher
Reclam turned the book down, he gave up further efforts. He wrote
to Russell that for the time being he was not going to take
further steps to have the book published, but that if Russell felt
like getting it printed the manuscript was at his disposal. Immediately afterwards Wittgenstein left Vienna and became a schoolmaster in the remote tiny village of Trattenbach in Lower Austria.

Russell had a typescript of the book. It was, moreover, the
only corrected and complete typescript. Wittgenstein had sent it
to Russell from the prison camp at Cassino. Later, after the book
had been printed, Wittgenstein gave it to his friend, Paul Engelmann. It is now in the Bodleian Library. For purposes of identifi-
cation I shall refer to it as the Engelmann typescript.

At that time Russell was about to embark on a journey to
China. Before leaving England he entrusted the typescript to
Miss Dorothy Wrinch with instructions to try to get it published.
Miss Wrinch first offered it to the Cambridge University Press.
When they turned it down in January 1921, she approached the
editors of three German periodicals. One flatly refused, and
another said he was willing to publish the paper later on, but asked
Miss Wrinch to return to the matter in May. Wilhelm Ostwald,

editor of the *Annalen der Naturphilosophie*, agreed to publish the paper without delay. He made it quite clear, however, that he too would have turned it down had it not been for his high regard for Bertrand Russell. Miss Wrinch dispatched the typescript to Ostwald in March. It appeared in the *Annalen* in the autumn of 1921. This was the final issue of Ostwald's journal.

Russell seems to have been unaware of these developments when he returned from China at the end of August and began to discuss publication of Wittgenstein's book in England with C. K. Ogden. Ogden had that very year assumed editorship of The International Library of Psychology, Philosophy and Scientific Method with the publishers Kegan Paul, Trench, Trubner & Co., Ltd. It is not known whether the idea that Wittgenstein's book might be included in that series came from the editor or from Russell. The earliest documents we have relating to this new turn in the history of how Wittgenstein's work got published is an undated letter from Miss Wrinch to Russell and a letter of 5th November 1921 from Ogden to Russell. The first refers to Ogden's interest in the matter, of which Russell evidently had told Miss Wrinch in an earlier letter. Ogden's letter to Russell, printed in Russell's *Autobiography*, reads as follows:

The International Library of
Psychology
Nov. 5, 1921

DEAR RUSSELL

Kegan Paul ask me to give them some formal note for their files with regard to the Wittgenstein rights.

I enclose, with envelope for your convenience, the sort of thing I should like. As they can't drop less than £50 on doing it I think it very satisfactory to have got it accepted – though of course if they did a second edition soon and the price of printing went suddenly down they might get their costs back. I am still a little uneasy about the title and don't want to feel that we decided in a hurry on *Philosophical Logic*. If on second thoughts you are satisfied with it, we can go ahead with that. But you might be able to excogitate alternatives that I could submit.

Moore's Spinoza title which he thought obvious and ideal is no use if you feel Wittgenstein wouldn't like it. I suppose his *sub specie aeterni*

in the last sentences of the book made Moore think the contrary, and
several Latin quotes. But as a selling title *Philosophical Logic* is better,
if it conveys the right impression.

Looking rapidly over the off print in the train last night, I was
amazed that Nicod and Miss Wrinch had both seemed to make so very
little of it.[1] The main lines seem so reasonable and intelligible – apart
from the Types puzzles. I know you are frightfully busy at present,
but I should very much like to know why all this account of signs and
symbols cannot best be understood in relation to a thoroughgoing
causal theory. I mean the sort of thing in the enclosed: – on "Sign
Situations" (= Chapter II of the early Synopsis attached). The whole
book which the publishers want to call *The Meaning of Meaning* is now
passing through the press; and before it is too late we should like to
have discussed it with someone who has seriously considered Watson.
Folk here still don't think there is a problem of *Meaning* at all, and
though your *Analysis of Mind* has disturbed them, everything still
remains rather astrological.

With best wishes for, and love to the family.

Yours sincerely

C. K. OGDEN

P.S. On second thoughts, I think that as you would prefer Wittgenstein's German to appear as well as the English, it might help if you
added the P.S. I have stuck in, and I will press them further if I can.

As Ogden's letter shows, by the beginning of November he
had studied an off-print of Ostwald's printing of the "Logisch-
philosophische Abhandlung". The words "Moore's Spinoza
title" in the letter must refer to the title *Tractatus Logico-Philosophicus*. It seems to have been first suggested by G. E. Moore. As
seen from his letter of 23rd April 1922 to Ogden (below, p. 20),
Wittgenstein preferred this Latin title to the alternative suggestion
Philosophical Logic.

Ogden's letter indicates that Russell was decidedly in favour of
printing the original German side by side with an English
translation. We know from a letter from Wittgenstein to Engelmann that the question of publication in both languages had in

---

[1] See *The Autobiography of Bertrand Russell, 1914–1944*, pp. 99–100.

fact already been discussed between Wittgenstein and Russell in December 1919 when they met in The Hague.[1]

Russell replied three days later to Ogden:

31 Sydney Str[eet]
[London,] S.W.3
8.11.1921

DEAR OGDEN,

I dare say I could part with Wittgenstein's MS without consulting him, but I thought it better to tell him what was being done. I wrote some days ago, and if I hear nothing by the end of next week I shall assume he has no objection. He certainly won't make a fuss anyhow, but I have as yet nothing definite *in writing* giving me the rights.

As for "philosophical logic", it seems to me all right, but if you like I will write to Wittgenstein and put alternatives before him.

I haven't had time to read your "Sign-Situations" yet, but I think probably the causal treatment of meaning does give the solution. It was because I thought so that I started working on "Analysis of Mind", which grew out of the problem of meaning.

Yours sincerely

BERTRAND RUSSELL

The words "part with Wittgenstein's MS" are slightly puzzling. They can hardly mean anything else than that Russell permitted Ogden to go ahead with publication. As far as we know, the only typescript which had been with Russell was the one Miss Wrinch had sent to Ostwald in February. It is possible that Ostwald returned it to Russell when the printing was completed. It was not, however, used for the printing in England. We do not know by whom and exactly when it was sent back to Wittgenstein. (See below, pp. 8–9.)

It seems that Wittgenstein had not heard even about the publication by Ostwald when he received the news from Russell about the plans for publication in England. His reply to Russell's letter is dated Trattenbach, 28th November:

---

[1] Paul Engelmann, *Letters from Ludwig Wittgenstein with a Memoir*, transl. by L. Furtmüller, Basil Blackwell, Oxford, 1967. Letter of 15th December 1919.

DEAR RUSSELL!

Many thanks for your kind letter! I must admit I am pleased that my stuff is going to be printed. Even though Ostwald is an utter charlatan. As long as he doesn't tamper with it! Are you going to read the proofs? If so, please take care that he prints it exactly as I have it. He is quite capable of altering the work to suit his own tastes – putting it into his idiotic spelling, for example. What pleases me most is that the whole thing is going to appear in England. I hope it may be worth all the trouble that you and others have taken with it.

You are right: the Trattenbachers are not uniquely worse than the rest of the human race. But Trattenbach is a particularly insignificant place in Austria and the *Austrians* have sunk so miserably low since the war that it's too dismal to talk about. That's what it is.

By the time you get this letter your child will perhaps already have come into this remarkable world. So: warmest congratulations to you and your wife! Forgive me for not having written to you for so long. I too haven't been very well and I've been tremendously busy. Please write again when you have time. I have not had a letter from Ostwald. If all goes well, I will come and visit you with the greatest of pleasure.

Kindest regards
Yours
LUDWIG WITTGENSTEIN[1]

After receipt of this letter, Russell wrote again to Ogden on 5th December, telling him that Wittgenstein had agreed to the publication plans.

31 Sydney Street
London, S.W.3
5.12.21

DEAR OGDEN,

Enclosed from Wittgenstein gives all the authority needed for going ahead, so you can tell the publishers it is all right. Please return Wittgenstein's letter to me, and let me see proof or typescript of Ostwald's stuff[2] if you have it. I am much relieved that W. takes the whole affair sanely.

All well here.
Yours
B. RUSSELL

[1] Translated by B. F. McGuinness.

[2] "Ostwald's stuff" can hardly mean anything else than the "*Logisch-philosophische Abhandlung*". The way Russell expresses himself here would indicate that *he* had not seen the off-print to which Ogden was referring in his letter of 5th November.

Ostwald also printed a German translation of Russell's Introduction to Wittgenstein's work. The translation was made from a typescript which Miss Wrinch had sent him with the typescript of the book. Ogden wanted to print the original of the Introduction with the new publication and wrote to Ostwald – only to find that he had destroyed the original. Ostwald's reply is dated 11th November:

Gross-Bothen
Königreich Sachsen
Landhaus Energie

Sehr geehrter Herr:

Ich bitte die Verzögerung meiner Antwort freundlichst zu entschuldigen: ich war verreist und dann unwohl.

Das Manuskript von B. Russells Einleitung kann ich leider nicht schicken, da ich es nicht mehr besitze. Ich hatte es aufbewahrt, bis ich die Korrektur der deutschen Übersetzung gelesen hatte; da es weiter nicht nötig war, ist es in den Papierkorb gewandert. Ich muss mit dem Entfernen von entbehrlichem Papier streng sein, da ich sonst in der Papierflut untergehen würde. Hätten Sie mir geschrieben, dass Sie das englische Manuskript zurück haben wollten, hätte ich es natürlich geschickt.

Sie können beliebig viele Exemplare von Wittgensteins Arbeit erhalten. Am einfachsten schreiben Sie deshalb an den Verlag Unesma, Leipzig, Kantstrasse 17. Von dort können Sie auch die deutsche Übersetzung von Russells Einleitung erhalten, nach der Sie den englischen Text nötigenfalls werden herstellen können.

Eine Übersetzung meiner Farbenlehre ins Englische beabsichtige ich nicht. Für Ihr freundliches Interesse danke ich Ihnen sehr.

Ihr ganz ergebener
W. Ostwald[1]

[1] Dear Sir,

I ask you kindly to forgive my delay in answering; I was away travelling and later unwell.

I regret that I cannot send the manuscript of B. Russell's Introduction, as I no longer have it. I kept it until I had read the proofs of the German translation; when it was no longer needed, it went into the wastepaper basket. I have to be strict in disposing of unnecessary paper, since otherwise I should be drowned in the flood of paper. Had you written to me that you wanted the English manuscript back, I should of course have sent it.

You can have as many copies as you want of Wittgenstein's work. The

Russell fortunately found a second copy and notified Ogden of this in an undated letter, evidently of mid-November.[1]

DEAR OGDEN

I have found a spare typescript of my introduction to Wittgenstein, which I enclose. So you needn't worry Ostwald about it any more.

Yours ever

B.R.

Later in the winter, however, Ogden seems to have returned the Introduction to Russell. For in a letter to Ogden of 9th May from Penzance Russell writes: "I return herewith the Introduction to Wittgenstein. I have added a page on p. 1, as you suggested." Actually, the printed Introduction is dated "May 1922". A comparison with the Ostwald printing shows that the English and the German versions for the most part correspond sentence by sentence except for some significant changes and additions in the beginning. These changes then were evidently made at Ogden's suggestion and the whole thing finished in May.

In Russell's letter of 9th May there is a puzzling passage. Russell says: "When you have proofs, I should be glad to see them with the MS I sent you, from which you have made the typescript." This would suggest that on the basis of the copy of the stuff which he had received in November Ogden made a typescript. If the second copy had been a manuscript and perhaps not easily legible, we could easily understand this. Russell indeed

---

simplest way is to write to the publisher, Verlag Unesma, Leipzig, Kant-strasse 17. From him you can also obtain the German translation of Russell's Introduction, from which you can, if necessary, reconstruct the English original.

I am not contemplating a translation into English of my Theory of Colours (*Farbenlehre*). I thank you very much for your kind interest in the matter.

Yours very sincerely

W. OSTWALD

[1] Ogden's reply in which he thanks Russell for the duplicate copy of the Introduction is likewise undated but refers to the arrival on the day of writing of Ostwald's above letter.

says it *was* a manuscript in his letter of 9th May. But in the letter from November quoted above he calls it a spare *typescript*.

The translation of the "Logisch-philosophische Abhandlung" into English was made in the course of the winter and completed by March. It seems that the first draft of the translation was produced by F. P. Ramsey alone. According to a statement by Ramsey's father in a memorial album composed and written after Ramsey's death in 1930 "he had been shown Wittgenstein's 'Tractatus' in MS or typescript and it interested him greatly. Then Ogden asked him to translate it for publication. His knowledge of German was so good that he used to go into Miss Pate's office and translate the book to a shorthand writer." Miss Pate was the head of the University Typing Office in Trinity Street, Cambridge. It is impossible to tell whether the typed text of the translation which still exists is the one produced in Miss Pate's office on the basis of Ramsey's dictation. The typescript was sent to Wittgenstein in March.

In a letter dated Trattenbach, 28th March, Wittgenstein acknowledges its receipt (see below, p. 17). It is plain from this letter that the typescript of the English translation was sent to him without the German text. Wittgenstein had at that time no typescript of his work with him. He could get one from Vienna, he says. But this would be an uncorrected (and hence incomplete) copy. The only corrected one, he reaffirms, is the copy he gave Russell, *i.e.* the copy I have called the Engelmann typescript. Wittgenstein wonders where it is now. He has heard nothing from Ostwald and even thinks Ostwald will not publish it. This is surprising, since it ought to have been plain from Russell's letter to him in November that Ostwald *was* printing the "Logisch-philosophische Abhandlung". (Russell's letter is not preserved; perhaps it had been unclear on this point.)

Wittgenstein's comments on specific points in the English translation show that he started correcting the translation before he had the German text in front of him (see pp. 41 and 42). But he evidently had access to the original at a later stage of the work. (See below, p. 43.)

We know that before returning the translation with his corrections and comments Wittgenstein had received an off-print of the Ostwald printing. Whether it was sent to him by Ogden or by Ostwald we do not know; probably he got it from the former. This off-print he returned to Ogden with his corrections at the same time as he returned the translation on 23rd April. (See below, p. 40.)

We do not know exactly when or from whom Wittgenstein also got back the Engelmann typescript from which Ostwald had printed the book. Perhaps he got it together with the off-print. The Engelmann typescript also contains numerous corrections which were made after it was printed. But it does not contain all the corrections which are in the off-print. It was evidently from this corrected off-print, and not from the Engelmann typescript, that the printing in England took place.

It is noteworthy that Wittgenstein, both in the letter of 28th March and in that of 23rd April and in his comments to 5.5542 (p. 34), speaks of "the translators" of his book in the plural. Since Ogden's letters to Wittgenstein have not been preserved, we do not know what Ogden had told Wittgenstein about the translating of the book. By "the translators" Wittgenstein can hardly have meant Ramsey and *Ogden*, since in the letter from April he asks Ogden to communicate his thanks to the translators. It must remain an open question whether there was someone else, whom we can no longer identify, who had assisted with the translating. Another possibility is that Ogden in his letter to Wittgenstein had said only that several persons had been involved in the job – meaning thereby Ramsey and himself and possibly also Russell. It is evident from the correspondence that Ogden was active in the translation.

In his letter to Engelmann of 15th December 1919, Wittgenstein hints that Russell was going to translate the book (and write an introduction to it). There is no direct evidence, however, that Russell had assisted in the production of the first draft of the translation in 1922. For it, Ramsey alone was probably responsible. (Cf. above, p. 8.) But in the typescript of the translation

which was sent to Wittgenstein in March there are some changes
which evidently had been made by Russell. Wittgenstein's comments to Ogden (below, pp. 28 and 31) show that he was aware
of this. But we have no contemporary evidence that Wittgenstein
had discussed directly with Russell details of the translation. It
is therefore surprising that Russell, in letters of a *much* later date,
1951 and 1960, explicitly refers to discussions with Wittgenstein
about the translation. In the first letter, to C. K. Ogden, Russell
says: "All that I do remember about the translation in general is
having arguments with Wittgenstein on various points, which
involved his sanctioning unliteral translations." The second
letter, to F. K. Ogden, reads as follows:

> Plas Penrhyn
> 21 November, 1960

I learn that questions have arisen as to the authenticity and authority
of the English version of Wittgenstein's *Tractatus*. I know that this
version was sanctioned point by point by Wittgenstein. There are
places where it is not an exact translation of the German. When I
pointed this out to him, he admitted it, but said that the translation as it
stood expressed what he wished to say better than a more exact
translation. It is, of course, open to anybody to make a new translation
in a more modern idiom, but it would be misleading to suggest that
such a translation gave a more accurate rendering of Wittgenstein's
thought at the time than that which was published. I say this from
recollection of careful and minute discussion with Wittgenstein as to
what he wished the English version to say.

> (signed) RUSSELL

The question arises: When and where did this "careful and
minute discussion with Wittgenstein" take place? It can hardly
have been in The Hague in 1919 when the translation had, for
all we know, not even been begun. For the first time after their
meeting in Holland, Russell and Wittgenstein met again at
Innsbruck in Austria between 6th and 11th August 1922. At
that stage Wittgenstein had already read and dispatched the
proofs of both the German and the English text back to Ogden.
(See below, pp. 57 and 58.) We do not know the topics of dis-

cussion at the meeting in Innsbruck. But it is at least a possibility that they concerned the translation and the forthcoming publication of the book in England.

The next exchange of letters between Ogden and Wittgenstein took place early in May. Ogden then sent Wittgenstein the Questionnaire, relating to specific points in the translation, which is here reproduced in facsimile. (There are also indications that he returned the typescript of the whole translation.) Wittgenstein sent back the Questionnaire with his annotations and comments. (See below, after p. 54.) In a letter a few days earlier Wittgenstein had replied to Ogden's request for more supplementary material to be printed with the book. (Below, p. 46.) It is not quite clear to me whether Ogden's request had been made in the same letter with which he sent the Questionnaire, or in a separate one.

In June Wittgenstein, at Ogden's request, sent to Ogden a declaration (see below, p. 55) whereby he gave the publisher Kegan Paul all the publication rights in his book. In the accompanying letter (below, p. 55) he discussed the question of complimentary copies. He asked Ogden to send one copy to the mother of David Pinsent, the friend to whose memory Wittgenstein had dedicated his work.

The next exchange of letters dates from July. Wittgenstein had left Trattenbach and was in Vienna. In his letter to Ogden, dated 17th July, he refers to Ogden's "good news" about the book. Perhaps the news was that proofs were now ready.

The proofs must have been dispatched some time in June or July. They were sent to Vienna, but forwarded from there to Hallein near Salzburg, where Wittgenstein was staying with relatives. He returned the proofs, duly corrected, on 4th August with a letter and a number of comments written on special sheets. (Below, p. 57ff.)

The final printing was evidently not made from the proofs Wittgenstein had corrected, but from a special set of proofs which somebody, probably Ogden himself, had prepared for the printer. This was natural, considering that the proofs which were sent to Austria contained comments and exchanges of questions and answers between Ogden and Wittgenstein in addition to the actual corrections.

Russell had been sent proofs of the book in June. In a letter, dated Penzance, 29th June, he says he is returning "the proofs of Wittgenstein". "I have corrected the Introduction but not his stuff, as I supposed you didn't need my help over that", he adds.

In a letter of 18th September (below, p. 67) Wittgenstein tells Ogden that he has now taken up a new post as schoolteacher. This was in Hasbach, another village in Lower Austria. Wittgenstein only stayed there a few weeks. Later that same autumn he moved to Puchberg am Schneeberg, where he stayed nearly two years.

The book was published in November. Ogden sent him the news and also some copies of the work. In a letter of 15th November Wittgenstein acknowledges receipt. Ogden also sent a copy to Pinsent's mother, who thanks him for it in a letter of 20th November and says she is going to write also to Wittgenstein. The other copies Wittgenstein seems to have given away to friends in Austria. It is not even certain that he kept a single copy for himself. In a letter to Professor Moritz Schlick, dated January 1925, he says explicitly that he himself had *no* copy of the book. (See also below, p. 71.)

In March 1923 Ogden and Wittgenstein again exchanged letters (below, p. 69f). *The Meaning of Meaning* by Ogden and I. A. Richards had just appeared and Ogden presented Wittgenstein with a copy.

When Wittgenstein submitted the *Tractatus* as a Ph.D. dissertation after his return to Cambridge in 1929, Ogden helped him to obtain a free copy of the book from the publishers. Wittgenstein, in a short note, expressed his gratitude.

Their last exchange of letters, as far as we know, took place in June 1933 when the second edition of the work was about to appear. (Below, p. 73f.)

The 1933 edition of the *Tractatus* incorporates a number of corrections by the author. Most of them had been made at a much earlier date, in September 1923, when F. P. Ramsey came to see Wittgenstein at Puchberg in Austria. Ramsey visited Austria again in the following year. An account of these visits and material relating to them is published here as an Appendix.

Letters from L. Wittgenstein to C. K. Ogden

1922–1933

with two sets of separate sheets of comments on the
English translation of the *Tractatus*

Words and phrases which Wittgenstein had underlined once are here set in *italics*, words and phrases twice underlined in SMALL CAPITALS, and words and phrases three times underlined in BIG CAPITALS.

Trattenbach bei Kirchberg a. Wechsel
Nieder-Österreich
28.3.1922

DEAR OGDEN!

Thanks so much for your letter and the translation. I will ret⟨o⟩urn it as soon as I have corrected it which I hope will be not later than in one or two weeks. It could be done quicker but I haven't got a copy of the German here and will have to wait till a copy of my M.S. is sent to me from Vienna which will take a few days. Now this brings me to a tremendous difficulty: I haven't got a CORRECTED copy of my book! – The only corrected copy there is I gave to Russell. But what on earth has happened to that? From your letter I gather that you haven't got it. Has Ostwald got it then? But he obviously doesn't think of printing my stuff, otherwise it would have appeared long ago! I have never had a line from Ostwald about it. (In fact I think he doesn't know my address and I don't know his.) Now if Ostwald has got my M.S. the only thing would be to get it back from him in order to print the German text. There can⟨n⟩'t be any good reason for letting him keep a M.S. which he will not publish. You will perhaps wonder why I don't sim[p]ly correct the copy which I have got but this I probably won't be able to do. That is to say: I can of course correct the spelling and rough mistakes, but the more subtle points of punctuation etc., which I have corrected in Ostwald['s] M.S. at a time when the matter was still alive in me, I can not correct now. And, besides, there are some additions I wrote into that M.S. which I don't know and of which – I think – I have got no copy. For correcting *the translation* my copy will do; for in the translation those more subtle points are lost at any rate. – I have now read through the translation once and have seen from it that there must be some awful⟨l⟩ faults in the German text the translators used. For the sense of some prop[osition]s is changed into the very reverse (of that I meant) in others it is destroyed al⟨l⟩together. However this can easily be mended!

But as to the German text I real[l]y don't know what to do. Please write to me as soon as you get this if you can get back my M.S. from Ostwald (D – HIM!) If not I will do my best to correct my copy and send it to you. I would of course regret⟨t⟩ VER⟨R⟩Y much if the German text was not printed in the English edition. – And now, my temper has cooled down a little by underlining three times the above curse, I can express my best thanks to you and to the translators who have taken a trouble which the whole thing – I'm af⟨f⟩raid – isn't worth. I am very sorry indeed to have to give you even more trouble yet for the reasons I mentioned. As to the translation I will ret⟨o⟩urn it to you with lots of notes which will enable you to find the ⟨w⟩right expression in such doubtful⟨l⟩ cases where I find the present expression wrong or awkward but am uncertain as to the correct English expression; in other cases where I knew how to correct the translation I have done it in the typewritten copy itself. In any case please look at all my corrections as I am never quite sure about English spelling – etc. and I hav[e]n't even got a dictionary.

Yours sincerely

LUDWIG WITTGENSTEIN

P.S. Is Johnson the logician still alive? If so, please remember me to him.

For the Editor's comments on this letter see also the Introduction.
Johnson. – W. E. Johnson (1858—1931), Fellow of King's College and Sidgwick Lecturer of Moral Science at Cambridge. Wittgenstein was very fond of Johnson, whom he knew from his pre-war Cambridge days, although he violently disagreed with Johnson's views on logic.

0.2   [Trattenbach]
23.4.1922

DEAR OGDEN,

Now I think I have finished the correction of both the German and the English text. I have taken great pains but especial[l]y as regards the English. I don't know if I have succeeded. It *is* a difficult business! Enclosed I am sending you 4 sheets with remarks on special points. Please kindly read them through carefully *every one* for there are some points in them which I think are rather important (as far as anything can be important in this affair).

Now I will make some general remarks first:

(1) The translation as you said, was in many points by far too literal. I have very often altered it such that now it doesn't seem to be a translation of the German at all. I've left out some words which occur in the German text or put in others which don't occur in the original etc. etc. But I al⟨l⟩ways did it in order to translate the *sense* (not the words).

(2) Wherever I made some alterations I have made a sign thus V at the margin in the same line in which the alteration was made. Likewise I made a V where I suggested some alteration in my remarks. And finally there are some V's to which there correspond no alterations or suggestions which I only made because I thought the translation *might* want altering and afterwards found out it didn't. – Thus in every line in which there is an alteration made or suggested in the remarks, there is a mark V, *but not vice versa.*

(3) It has happened several times that I altered the translation and found out afterwards that the translation had been all right as it was. Then I crossed out my alteration and put a sign thus ...... underneath the original translation, as much as to say "I beg your pardon, it was all right".

(4) Wherever there occur symbols which are not my own invention they should be Russell[']s. In my typescript I have used others, only because Russell[']s symbols could very often not be typed and I was too lazy to put them in afterwards. Thus where I used "/" for "not" put Russell[']s " ~ "; where I used "C" for

"implies" put Russell[']s "⊃". When signs like "fa" or "fx" occur I very often wrote "f(a)" or "f(x)" in the original but I am now leaving the brackets out. So whenever "f(x)" occurs I've crossed the brackets out thus "f⦗x⦘" which means that the sign is to be printed "fx" simply.

(5) The signs „–" (I don't know what you call them) I have very often written as I am accustomed in German thus „–" instead of thus "–". So wherever I have written them wrongly just put them right.

(6) I had rather not use Italics where latin phrases occur for the very reason you mentioned. Otherwise the use of Italics and quotation marks (that's the word) was all right except where I have altered it.

(7) I have read through your remarks carefully. My answers to them are embodied in *my* remarks. Where there is no answer this means that the translation is allright as it is.

(8) As to ⊂⊃ you will see from my correction as well as from the German that the prop[osition] had been mutilated. The figure s⟨c⟩hould be like this ⊂⊃ and not ◁ ; because this is how people very often imagine the shape of the field of vision to be. This, by the way, has *nothing whatever* to do with light going in strai[gh]t lines.

I'm sorry I am giving you so much trouble with those silly figures, symbols etc. etc., but I don't know how to help it! – Unless by leaving out some prop[osition]s and *writing in a footnote that something has been left out.*

(9) As to the title I think the latin one is better than the present title. For al⟨l⟩though "Tractatus logico-philosophicus" isn't *ideal* still it has something like the right meaning, whereas "Philosophic logic" is wrong. In fact I don't know what it means! There is no such thing as philosophic logic. (Unless one says that as the whole book is nonsense the title might as well be nonsense too.)

(10) Wherever I want to begin a new line where there is none in

the typescript yet I put a bracket [. And where I want a line to begin⟨n⟩ further to the right I made a sign thus [→.

(11) I sup[p]ose I needn't mention that my preface must be printed *immediately* before the main text and *not* as in Ostwald[']s edition Russell[']s Introduction in between the preface and the book!

(12) As in the preface there are no numbers I have for the sake of reference written 1,2,3,4,5,6, on such lines about which I made a remark. The first remark I made to No 3. Of course these numbers must not be printed.

(13) The word "Sachlage" has been translated "state of affairs". Now I don't like this translation but don't know what to suggest in its place. I have thought of the latin "status rerum" (?) would this be better? –

Now I can⟨n⟩'t think of any more remarks. I hope I may have succeeded in making myself understood. If my explanations are rather lengthy please excuse this. I don't mind so much if they are tiresom[e] if only they are CLEAR.

I now understand that the translators must have had an awful⟨l⟩ job. Please give them my best thanks, they have done their work excel[l]ent⟨e⟩ly. I wish I had done mine half as well.

I, too, hope we may meet again some day.

Yours sincerely

LUDWIG WITTGENSTEIN

P.S. Please begin⟨n⟩ each number as you did in the typescript in the way one general[ly] begin⟨n⟩s a new line and not as Ostwald did.

---

4 sheets with remarks. – These amount in fact to 5 sheets of 4 pages each, i.e. to 20 foolscap pages. Perhaps "4" is a slip of the pen for "5".

The √ signs. Ogden ticked them off when checking the places. In the typescript as we have it they therefore usually appear as √.

Russell's symbols. – Ostwald had printed the symbols just as they stood in the typescript which gives the Ostwald text a very odd appearance.

The signs ,,–". – The conventional way of printing quotation marks in German differs from the standard way in English. Cf. the printed text of the *Tractatus.*

meet again some day. – Wittgenstein and Ogden had met at Cambridge before the war. An undated note, perhaps from the late 1920's, would indicate that the two men also met later, after Wittgenstein's return to Cambridge. See below *O.13*, p. 72.

P.S. – Wittgenstein means that the first line of each remark should be indented to the right. In the Ostwald printing the first lines are not indented.

3 instead of: "to be set a limit" I propose "to draw a limit".

4   „   „ "be set in"   „   "be drawn in".

5 leave out "whatever".

6 On the other hand the truth of the thought communicated here seems to me unassailable. . . .

Leave out the title on the first page where I have crossed it out.

1.11   ". . . by the facts, and by these being *all* the facts" or ". . . [by the facts,] and in that these are . . ." isn't the first alternative better?

2.011   wouldn't it be English to say ". . . a thing that it *can* be a constituent part . . ." instead of "that it s⟨c⟩hould be able . . ."? If the first isn't awkward please put it in.

2.0121   "gleichsam" doesn't mean "likewise" (this means gleichfalls). The prop[osition] s⟨c⟩hould be something like: "It would, $\begin{Bmatrix} \text{so to speak} \\ \text{as it were} \end{Bmatrix}$, appear as an accident . . .". "Verband" in the end of the prop[osition] means "context" not "connexion". I hope it is all right as I have corrected it.

2.02331   Instead of "otherwise it is distinguished" put "for otherwise it $\begin{Bmatrix} \text{would be} \\ \text{were} \end{Bmatrix}$ distinguished".

2.03   Here instead of "hang one on another" it should be "hang one in another" as the links of a chain *do*! The meaning is *that there isn't anything third* that connects the links but that the links *themselves* make connexion with one another. So if "in" in this place is English please put it there. If one would hang *on* the other they might also be glued together.

2.15   "its" in the last line means *the picture*[']*s*. If this isn't clear put "the form of representation of the picture".

2.1515   Here by "Fühler" I meant the things which a butterfly has. If these are called "feelers" its all right.

2.22   Should it not be "fals[e]hood" rather than "falsity"?

3.001   I don't know how to translate this. The German "Wir können uns ein Bild von ihm machen" is a phrase commonly used. I have rendered it by "we can imagine it" because "imagine" comes from "image" and this is something like picture. In German it is a sort of pun you see.

In 3.141 I should propose to put "mixture" instead of "medley". What this proposition means is that propositions do not consist of words in *that* sense in which a colour which a painter uses consists of different tints. I.e. that the prop[osition] isn't a mixture of words in the sense in which a colour may be a mixture of other colours. The main stress does NOT lie on the point that the proposition isn't a disordered higgledy[-]piggledy sort of combination of words, but merely on the point that it is no MIXTURE at all but a STRUCTURE.

In the end of that prop[osition] couldn't one say "is articulate" instead of "articulated"? I didn't mean yet to say that the prop[osition] is articulatED but I used the word "artikuliert" in the sense in which one might say that a man speaks articulate that is that he pronounces the words distinctly. Or do you in that case also say "articulated"? If so leave it as it stands if not you put "articulate".

3.251   About this prop[osition] please consider what I said about 3.141

HERE TWO PAGES HAVE TO BE INTERCHANGED

3.3   Put "context" instead of "connexion" if that's English.

3.317   At the end of this prop[osition] there is something left out. The German of it is: "wie die Beschreibung der Sätze geschieht, ist unwesentlich" (This – by the way –

begins a new line.) English: "The way in which we describe the propositions is unessential."

3.322   Shouldn't it be: ". . . and where would then be what was common in the symbolisation?"?

3.323   Instead of ". . . of the fact that *something* happens." I would rather write ". . . of *something* happening."

3.325   Wouldn't it be better to put instead of "sign language" "symbolism"?

3.327   I propose: "The sign determines a logical form only together with it's logical . . .."

3.328   Here I made the translation more explicit than the German text. (The original translation was quite wrong.)

3.3421 Isn't "symbolisation" clumsy? Wouldn't "symbolising" be better? I am not sure.

3.42   "The logical scaffolding round the picture determines the logical space" isn't right. It should be rather ". . . round the picture reaches through the whole logical space" which means that the scaffolding is as big as the logical space. You could imagine a house with such a big scaffolding round it that by its length, breadth and width it filled the whole space. (Though "filling" wouldn't be the right expression. I think to "reach through space" is what I mean.)

4.002   "From it is humanly impossible . . ." oughtn't it to be "From it it is humanly . . ." or "It is humanly impossible to gather from it immediately the logic . . .". Or is "to gather" not English in this context?

4.01   "As we think of it" isn't what I mean. What I mean is, roughly speaking, that a prop[osition] is a model of reality as we imagine it (i.e. as we imagine reality).

4.011   The end of this prop[osition] ought to be (I think): "And yet these $\left\{\begin{array}{l}\text{sign-languages}\\\text{symbolisms}\end{array}\right\}$ prove to be pictures – even in the ordinary sense of the word – of $\left\{\begin{array}{l}\text{the things}\\\text{what}\end{array}\right\}$ they represent". (I like the second alternatives better.)

4.012   "aRb" not "a Rb".

4.014   Ought it not to be ". . . all stand to one another in that pictorial . . ."?

4.0141   There was a supplement bound with the M.S. Ostwald has got and in this there are prop[osition]s of which I wasn't sure w[h]ether I should incorporate them into my work or not. In fact *only one* has been taken into the book and that was the N° 72 which runs: "Daß es eine allgemeine Regel gibt, durch die der Musiker aus der Partitur die Symphonie entnehmen kann, durch welche man aus der Linie auf der Grammophonplatte die Symphonie und nach der ersten Regel wieder die Partitur ableiten kann, darin besteht eben die innere Ähnlichkeit dieser scheinbar so ganz verschiedenen Gebilde. Und jene Regel ist das Gesetz der Projektion, welche die Symphonie in die Notensprache projiziert. Sie ist die Regel der Übersetzung der Notensprache in die Sprache der Grammophonplatte." In English: "In the fact that there is a general rule by which the musician is able to read the symphony out of the score, and that there is a rule by which one could reconstruct the symphony from the line on a gram⟨m⟩ophon[e] record and from this again – by means of the first rule – construct the score, herein lies the internal similarity between these things which at first sight ⟨are⟩ seem to be entirely different. And the rule is the law of projection which projects the symphony into the language of the musical score. It is the rule of translation of this language into the language of the gram⟨m⟩ophon[e] record."

4.015   Here instead of ["]likenesses["] the plural form of "simile" would – I think – be better. This prop[osition] in English seems to me very awkward and unclear but I can't mend it. Would it perhaps be better to put instead of ". . . of the whole pictorial nature . . ." "of all the imagery of our language"?

4.022   2nd line. This ought to be something like: "The prop-

[osition] *shows* how things stand, *if* it is true. And it *says*, that so they stand." The German "wie es sich verhält, wenn . . ." is quite a general expression for any fact; it does not mean things are connected etc.⟨.⟩

4.023   This prop[osition] I cannot translate. The present translation is WRONG. The meaning of it should be that a prop[osition] determines reality such that by merely affirming or denying it one can make it agree with reality. A prop[osition] can⟨n⟩'t entirely determine reality for it al⟨l⟩ways can either be true or false; but it can ONLY be true or false. That means the prop[osition] determines reality *so far* that one only needs to say "yes" or "no" to it, and nothing more, to make it agree with reality. It is like fixing – say – a shelf on the wall with *one* nail and saying: now this is fixed so far that I only need turn it this or that way and it will be right. What I have here underlined thus ⸍⸍⸍⸍⸍⸍ or something like it might serve as a translation if nothing better is suggested.

The second part: "It must therefore be completely described . . ." is all right.

In the end of this prop[osition] "how everything logical is connected" is wrong. "*Es verhält sich* so und so" does not mean "things are connected such and such" (see Nº 4.022) but it is a general expression like "such and such *is the case*"! One might translate it freely thus: ". . . and therefore one can actually see in the prop-[osition] all the logical features of reality if it is true."

4.025   Instead of "And the dictionary translates not only . . ." wouldn't it be better: "And the dictionary doesn't only translate . . ."?

4.032   Here "articulated" is right!

4.04   This doesn't seem to me quite clear. I think it would be clearer what was meant if it ran: ". . . there must be exactly as many things distinguishable as . . ." although this is rather clumsy. But it gives the right meaning.

4.062   Instead of "Can we not come to an understanding ..."
I propose "Can we not make ourselves understood by
means of false prop[osition]s ...". This seems to me to
give the meaning more correctly but I'm not sure. Here
again "wenn es sich so verhält ..." doesn't mean "if
things are so connected".

4.112   Isn't clarification a very clumsy word? Especially in its
second occurrence. Couldn't one say: "...but the get[t]ing
clear of propositions." Or is this still more awkward?

4.12   Here in the 2nd line I should leave the "the" out, but as
Russell has put it in I didn't dare to strike it out.

4.1211   Instead of "... that mention is made of the same object
in them both." I propose "... that they are both about
the same object."

4.122   "The existence of such ..." seems wrong. That a
relation exists cannot be asserted at all. What we can
assert is that it *holds* between certain objects. So put
"holding" instead of "existence" or something synony-
mous.

4.123   Should it not be "(Here to the shifting use of the
words "property" and "relation" there corresponds
the shifting use ..." instead of "(Here there corresponds ..."?

4.1252   It would be clearer if the terms of the series "aRb",
"(Ex) : aRx.xRb" etc. were printed one *below* the other
thus:

"aRb"
"(Ex) : aRx.xRb"
"(Ex,y) : aRx.xRy.yRb"
etc.

4.126   Instead of "number sign" put either "sign of number"
or "numerical sign".
"Denn ihre Merkmale, die formalen Eigenschaften...".
Here the word "Merkmal" is taken from Frege[']s
terminology. He calls "Merkmale" of a concept the
properties which a thing must have in order to fall under

the concept as an object belonging to it. – Now I don't know if one can here translate "Merkmal" by "characteristic". Russell is sure to know the proper translation of "Merkmal" in the above sense. The same applies in a later part of this prop[osition].

4.1272 Couldn't "Scheinbegriff" be translated by "pseudo-concept"?

And later on in the same prop[osition] instead of "apparent propositions" couldn't it be "pseudopropositions" or is this clumsy?

Instead of " 'There are X objects' " it must be " 'There are $\aleph_0$ objects' " where $\aleph_0$ is a Hebrew letter *Aleph* with the suffix o used in mathematics for an infinite number. I am not sure – however – if I write it correctly. It also occurs in the "Principia Mathematica".

4.128   Here the word[s] "special numbers" does not give the right meaning, I think. What I meant was that in Logic there are no numbers which are in any sense more important or of any greater significance, in any sense preeminent, as compared with the rest of numbers. Such for instance many people believe that the number *one* is such a number or the number 3. And if – for instance – there was in Logic a definite number of primitive prop[osition]s or of primitive ideas – say the number one or any other – then this number would have, in some sense, to *prevail* all through logic and consequently also throughout philosophy. It would then be a number more important than the rest, an "ausgezeichnete Zahl". I have put "preeminent" instead of special. If this won't do please alter it. (But don't leave "special".)

4.28   Wouldn't "falsehood" be better than "falsity"? I don't know. The same applies to 4.41 etc.

4.411   "von vornherein" doesn't mean "a priori". It should be something like: "It is probable from the very beginning that the bringing in of . . ." or "It seems probable even on first sight . . .".

4.442   Instead of "proposition sign" put "propositional sign" or "sign of a proposition".

4.464   Here as in the preceding prop[osition] there is a great difficulty about the use of "the". I would rather leave it out altogether before "tautology" and "contradiction". But if this is impossible rather put "a" instead of "the". So 4.464 would be: "The truth of tautology is certain, of propositions possible, of contradiction impossible." Here I have put "tautology" and "contradiction" in the SINGULAR and "propositions" in the *plural* deliberately because there are in fact no contradictions but there is only contradiction, for they all mean the same, *i.e.* nothing. And the same applies to tautology.

4.5   Instead of ". . . which falls under the description" put ". . . which conforms to the description" or "which satisfies the description" or something like this.

4.5   In the end of this prop[osition] "Es verhält sich so und so" doesn't mean "Things are combined in such and such a way" but – as I have mentioned above – it means something like "such and such is the case". This is the only English expression I know for it. Perhaps one could say "things stand such and such". The expression must be one used in every day language to express that something or other is the case.

5.101   Here the symbols in brackets on the *right hand side* (i.e. the symbols which *follow* the *words*) should be printed in Russell[']s *symbolism* as used in the PRINCIPIA MATHE-MATICA. In my M.S. they are different only because one couldn't write them otherwise with the type-writer. The prop[osition]s in Russell[']s symbolism⟨e⟩ should be in square brackets. Thus:
"(TTTT)(p,q) Tautology (p implies p, and q implies q) $[p \supset p . q \supset q]$
(FTTT)(p,q) in words: Not both p and q $[\sim (p.q)]$"
The *expressions in words are not put in brackets except* in the

case of tautology and contradiction where they have to stand in round brackets as they do.

5.12 Your correction, the transposition of "first" and "second", is quite right. Is "first" and "second" in the wrong order in the German too? If so, please set it right. Otherwise leave the German as it is.

5.1311 Here as in the whole book the symbolisms for "not" ($\sim$) and "or" ($\vee$) should be Russell[']s (Principia Math.). As symbol for "neither p nor q" please use "p|q". So *that* part of the prop[osition] becomes: "But if we write e.g. instead of "p $\vee$ q" "p|q.|.p|q" and instead of "$\sim$p" "p|p" (p|q = neither p nor q) . . .". So don't use shrieks in the printing but simply upright dashes "|". I used "!" only because I had no other type for it.

5.1361 "Belief in the causal nexus is superstition" isn't right. It ought to be: "Superstition is the belief in the causal nexus". I didn't mean to say that the belief in the causal nexus was one amongst superstitions but rather that superstition is nothing else than the belief in the causal nexus. In the German this is expressed by the definite article before "Aberglaube".

5.143 Here in the first line I first crossed out Russell[']s note but found afterwards that I could think of no better translation myself.

In the second and third occurrence of "contradiction" and "tautology" in this prop[osition] the article in English must, I think, be left out altogether to give the right meaning. It *may* be left out in the first occurrence too.

5.252 Isn't "Only so . . ." awkward? Wouldn't "Only thus . . ." or "Only in this way . . ." be better?

5.42 Here the symbols should be Russell[']s as above. The same applies to 5.43 where it should be "$\sim\sim$p" instead of "||p" etc. etc.

5.43 "von vornherein" doesn't mean "a priori" but something like "from the very beginning" but here you had better leave it out al⟨l⟩together in the translation.

5.441   Here the symbols ought to be "$\sim$(Ex).$\sim$fx" and "(Ex).fx.x$=$a".

5.451   Here my correction (striking out "the same thing by" etc.) seems wrong *but it is all right*! What the translation said was *quite true but it didn't say what I meant*.

5.452   In the 3rd line from below is it English to say ". . . has proved itself necessary . . ."? Should it not be ". . . has proved necessary . . ." or ". . . has proved to be necessary . . ." or "has turned out to be necessary . . ."?

5.453   About the prop[osition] "Es gibt keine ausgezeichneten Zahlen" I have made my remarks above. Please translate it as in its first occurrence (4.128). I propose "There are no preeminent numbers" but perhaps there is something better for it.

5.461   ". . . is full of significance." Isn't this very awkward? Wouldn't it be better to say ". . . is of great importance." or something like this?

5.473   Here the last line but one seems to me wrong. It should – I think – be something like: ". . . but not because of the symbol being unpermissible in itself." For the symbol *is* as a matter of fact *not* unpermissible. Whereas from the English as it stands it would appear as if the symbol was unpermissible and as if all I wanted to say was that the senselessness of the proposition didn't arise from the use of that unpermissible symbol. In German my meaning is expressed by the use of "wäre" (*conjunctive mood*).

5.4731 I think in the end it ought to be "illogically" instead of "unlogically". But I'm not certain.

5.4733 I know that "legitimately" instead of "rightly" seems very awkward but I think this can⟨n⟩'t be helped here.

5.5   In the expression "(. . . T)(ζ . . .)" the space between the two brackets should be not larger than in the symbol "(TTTT)(p,q)" etc. in the prop[osition] 5.101. It is all right in the German text.

5.513   If "What is common . . ." isn't good English put "that which is in common . . ." instead; but *not* "the common element . . .".

5.514   last line: wouldn't "is mirrored" be better than "mirrors itself"?

5.5261   This would be clearer if the prop[osition] in brackets was "(This is shown by the fact that in "(Ex, ϕ).ϕx" we must mention "ϕ" and "x" separately.)". Please put it thus.

5.535   I propose "pseudopropositions" instead of "apparent propositions".

4.003   The end of this prop[osition] has been left out. It begins a new line and runs thus:

"Und es ist nicht verwunderlich, dass die tiefsten Probleme eigentlich *keine* Probleme sind."

English something like: "And it isn't to be wondered at that the deepest problems are real[l]y *no* problems.

This comes after ". . . is more or less identical than the beautiful⟨1⟩."

5.25   Wouldn't it be better to put "only its result does" instead of "only its result does that".

5.542   ". . . via co-ordination . . .", I think, is wrong. It ought to be something like ". . . coordination of facts by means of a coordination of their objects."

5.5423   Should it not be ". . . that its constituents are combined in such . . ." instead of ". . . are combined together in such . . ."?

5.552   ". . . that things are combined in such and such a way . . ." is wrong (as twice before). It should be something like: ". . . that such and such is the case . . .".

5.551   "And if we get into a situation where we need to answer . . .". If this is too clumsy, simply put "And if we ever need to answer . . .".

5.553   Here instead of "special" you will have to put the same as in N° 4.128 and N° 5.453.

5.5542   "May we not then ask . . .". I think "not" ought to be left out. Because the correct answer to this question would be, that we may NOT! Whereas as the translators put it one would expect the answer: we *may*.

5.61   (last line) ". . . therefore also say" seems to me quite unenglish. If it real[l]y is so, simply leave it out. Or would it be correct to say: "we cannot therefore *say* either what we cannot think"? I would have put it that way but I don't know if it's English.

5.62   Isn't "to deciding" clumsy? But I don't know what to suggest instead.

6   I think "the" can be simply left out. If not, put "propositionS" and "functionS" and have the "the" out in any case.

6.111   Last 2 lines: Instead of ". . . and this is a certain sign of the fact that it was falsely conceived" I propose ". . . and this is a $\left\{\begin{array}{l} \text{certain} \\ \text{safe} \end{array}\right\}$ symptom of it be⟨e⟩ing falsely understood."

6.121   "This method could be called a null-method." "Null-methode" in German is an expression used in physics; when – for instance – you measure an electric resistance by regulating another resistance until⟨l⟩ the galvanometer points to o again we call this a "Nullmethode". Now there is sure to be an English word for it; but is it "null-method"? It should rather be "zero-method" but I don't know.

6.2341   This prop[osition] now begin⟨n⟩s in German: "Das Wesentliche der mathematischen Methode ist es, mit Gleichungen zu arbeiten."

6.31   Is the end of this prop[osition] English as I have put it? If not, leave the "either" out.

6.341   "Whatever kind of picture appears I can . . ." This is not clear. It must be something like: "Whatever kind of picture these (the spots) give . . ." or "Whatever kind of picture thereby appears on the white surface . . ." or something of that sort.

6.342   Instead of "But *this* is what characterises the picture, the fact . . ." I would like to translate "But this *does* characterise the picture . . .". This has a slightly different sense and if it is English please put it thus.

6.3431 Instead of "throughout" it must be "through". The word is used here in the same sense as when I say "I speak through a tube" or "I hear his voice through the wall" etc.

6.361 "Only uniform connexions are thinkable". "uniform", I think, is wrong. To get the right expression please look up the English translation of Hertz's "Principles of Mechanics". In the German text it is *"gesetzmäßige Zusammenhänge"*.

6.362 Wouldn't it be better thus: "What can be described can happen too, and . . ."?

6.372 This is wrong, it should be something like: "So people stop at the natural laws as at something . . .". The prop[osition] means that people don't enquire any further, their investigations STOP there as if they now had explained everything.

6.41 ". . . and if there were, it would have no value." I would propose ". . . and if there were, it would be of no value." This seems to me better and gives my meaning. Analogously in the next line instead of ". . . which has value . . ." I would put ". . . which is of value . . .".

6.43 Last line but one: Isn't it possible to leave "man" out?

6.4311 Last line: Instead of "limitless" I propose "without limit". The German "grenzenlos" is quite a usual expression whereas "limitless" in English, I think, is not.

6.4312 Now here that part of the translation which I have crossed out, al⟨l⟩though it was much better English than what *I* wrote on top of it, was wrong. But it is very difficult to explain wherein the fault lies. My translation, too, is not good, and if it is *too* awkward please put something else instead of it. The meaning of the German phrase I will try to explain: If for instance one tries to prove a proposition in Physics we make certain assumptions and hope that they will do our business, i.e. that they will prove the point in question, i.e. that from them our proposition will follow. Now if we find that it doesn't follow then what we will say about our assumptions is exactly what I tried to express. I think one would say something like: "These assumptions will not do our business" or "they will not prove what we tried to prove with them" but we wouldn't say "they will not effect what we wished to attain by them". If my translation won't do perhaps the best thing will be to make the statement more explicit in the English and write: ". . . but this assumption . . . will not solve the problem for us which $\begin{Bmatrix} \text{men} \\ \text{we} \end{Bmatrix}$ al⟨l⟩ways $\begin{Bmatrix} \text{tried to} \\ \text{would} \end{Bmatrix}$ solve by it" or something of that sort.

There is another difficulty about this prop[osition] still. "*Rätsel*" has been translated with "riddle". Now I don't know if this is right. Possibly it is. The word "Rätsel" in German has two meanings. Such e.g. "why is a raven like a writing desk[?]" we call a *Rätsel*. But we also talk of, say, the "Rätsel des menschlichen Lebens" or of the "Rätsel der Existenz der Welt" etc. and here the word "Rätsel" has a different meaning, it has a higher meaning. Now do you use "riddle" in this second sense also? IF SO, IT IS QUITE RIGHT. Only I don't w⟨h⟩ish that there should be anything ridiculous or profane or frivolous in the word when used in the connection "riddle of life" etc.

6.4321   Here "task" was all right but I'm not sure if "solution" is the right word. If e.g. you tell a man to dig a hole, then if he digs it, is the digging of it called the "solution" of the task you give him? If so, "solution" is the right word.

6.44   I don't like "mystical element". I suppose one can⟨n⟩'t say in English "the mystical" simply. If so, I would like it better.

6.45   Here "mystical element" is *wrong*! If anything, it must be "mystical feeling" for in *this* prop[osition] the German "das mystiche" is an adjective belonging to "Gefühl".

6.5   "*The riddle*". Here "The" must be printed in italics too. It means as much as "the riddle 'par excellence' ". As to the word "riddle" see above.

6.52   Is "be" right instead of "are" or should it be "were"? Al⟨l⟩though in German I did not use the conjunctive mood, I think in English "be" comes nearer to the real meaning.

6.522 "the mystical element". This is the same case as in 6.44 but *not* the same as in 6.45.

3,4,5,6, The numbers refer to the English translation of the Preface. (See above, p. 21.) The manuscript or typescript no longer exists. The numbers 3, 4, and 5 correspond to the paragraphs of the Preface. The number 6 is perhaps a slip of the pen for 8. The printed text agrees with Wittgenstein's suggestions. In the proofs Wittgenstein changed the occurrence of the word "truth" in the sentence beginning "On the other hand . . ." to italics.

1.11 The first alternative was adopted.

2.011 Wittgenstein's suggestion was adopted.

2.0121 The alternative "so to speak" was chosen and Wittgenstein's correction of "connexion" to "context" was observed. The use, here and elsewhere, of curly brackets and of underlining ~~~~ is Wittgenstein's. Under the alternatives in brackets he had written here "choose between the two"; in 2.02331 he wrote "I don't know which is correct".

In this remark Wittgenstein also made a few other changes to the translation. The first sentence ran in the original translation "It appears likewise as an accident, when a thing that could exist alone on its own account, is subsequently fitted into a state of affairs." Wittgenstein changed this to "It would, so to speak, appear as an accident, when to a thing that could exist alone on its own account, subsequently a state of affairs could be made to fit." In the second paragraph of the remark he changed "A logical entity cannot be only-possible." to "A logical entity cannot be merely possible." In the last paragraph he substituted "the context of" for "connexion with" and, at the very end, "context" for "connexion".

2.02331 Wittgenstein's suggestion was adopted.

2.03 Wittgenstein's suggestion was adopted.

2.15 Ogden followed Wittgenstein's suggestion.

2.22 Ogden printed "falsehood".

3.001 The translation originally was: "'An atomic fact is thinkable' – means: we can make for ourselves a picture of it.' Ogden printed in accordance with Wittgenstein's suggestion.

3.141 Ogden adopted Wittgenstein's suggestions.

3.251 Here too the original "articulated" was corrected to "articulate".

"HERE TWO . . .". It is no longer possible to determine what this refers to. Presumably two pages in the typescript of the English translation with which Wittgenstein was working had had their order reversed.

3.3   Wittgenstein's suggestion was adopted.

3.317   The last paragraph of this remark had been left untranslated. Ogden printed it as suggested by Wittgenstein but changed "unessential" to "not essential".

3.322   In the original translation the word "then" occurred after "symbolisation". Wittgenstein suggested that it be placed after "would". Ogden placed it before the "would" which makes the sentence English.

3.323   Ogden followed Wittgenstein's suggestion.

3.325   Ogden followed Wittgenstein's suggestion.

3.327   Ogden followed Wittgenstein's suggestion. The original translation had "primarily in conjunction with" instead of "only together with".

3.328   The comment concerns the second paragraph of this remark. The German is: "(Wenn sich alles so verhält als hätte ein Zeichen Bedeutung, dann hat es auch Bedeutung.)". The original translation rendered this by "(If everything is combined as though a sign had meaning, then it has meaning.)". Wittgenstein changed this to "(If everything in the symbolism works as though a sign had meaning, then it has meaning.)". This last version was printed.

3.42   Wittgenstein crossed out the comments on this remark – probably because he realized that the last sentence of the remark under discussion takes care of the point he had made in the comment.

3.3421   The printed text has "symbolizing".

4.002   Ogden printed "From it it is humanly impossible to gather immediately the logic of language.". The translation originally had "to understand" instead of "to gather".

4.01   The passage under discussion had been translated "The proposition is a model of the reality, as we think of it.". In the typescript Wittgenstein changed this to "The proposition is a model of the reality as we think it is.". This is how Ogden printed it.

4.011   Of the alternatives Ogden chose "symbolisms" and "what".

4.014   The original translation had "another" in place of "one another".

4.0141   The typescript had against this number the words "(See Supplement No. 72)". This was evidently a translation of the

corresponding place in the Ostwald printing "(Siehe Ergänzung Nr. 72)". This seems virtually conclusive evidence for the
conjecture that the English translation was made from an
off-print of the Ostwald printing and not from the typescript
from which Ostwald had printed. In this typescript of his
work (see above, p. 26) Wittgenstein has inserted in longhand
the words "4.0141 (Siehe Ergänzung Nr. 72)" after the
remark 4.014. The "Ergänzung" itself is typed on two small
slips of paper attached to the end of the entire typescript. In
the off-print of the Ostwald printing which Wittgenstein
returned to Ogden with his corrections, the remark is written
in Wittgenstein's hand on a slip of paper which is attached to
the appropriate page in the off-print. In the proofs of the
parallel edition which were later sent to Wittgenstein, the
German version of 4.0141 is printed, but the English version
is typed on an inserted slip of paper. This is a little surprising,
and I cannot think of a reason for this discrepancy between
the German and the English proofs at this point. It is of some
interest to note that the translation of this remark is entirely
by Wittgenstein himself. (On the supplements, see also below
p. 46.) Wittgenstein gives us to understand that all the supplements, of which there were about a hundred, were originally
attached to the German (Engelmann) typescript. The typescript as it now exists has only this particular supplement 72
attached to it. It is a reasonable conjecture that Wittgenstein
removed the other supplements and destroyed them before
giving the typescript to Engelmann.

4.015   Wittgenstein's suggestions were accepted. The remark had
originally been rendered as follows: "The possibility of all
likenesses, of the whole of the pictorial nature of our manner
of expression, rests on the logic of representation."

4.022   The second paragraph in this remark had been translated as
follows: "The proposition *shews* how things are connected,
if it is true. And it *says*, that things are so connected." It is
printed in the form: "The proposition *shows* how things stand,
if it is true. And it *says*, that they do so stand." It is of some
interest to note that the translator had originally used the form
"shew" and not "show". The fact that the "shew" is not
corrected (in the typescript) and that the proofs have "show"
would indicate either that the correction was made by the
printer from the galley or that the proofs were set on the basis
of a different typescript from that which Wittgenstein returned.
However, no such other typescript has been found.

4.023   The original translation of the passage under discussion was: "The reality must be determined by the proposition: affirmatively or negatively". The way in which it was eventually printed is "The proposition determines reality to this extent, that one only needs to say "Yes" or "No" to it to make it agree with reality." The way Wittgenstein here quotes from the typescript which has corrections in Ogden's hand clearly shows that Ogden had made changes in the original translation *before* he sent the typescript on to Wittgenstein.

At the end of the remark the translation originally was "one can actually see in the proposition how everything logical is connected if it is true". The printed version is "one can actually see in the proposition all the logical features possessed by reality if it is true".

4.025   Wittgenstein's suggestion was adopted.

4.032   Cf. above, p. 24, comment on 3.141.

4.04   Wittgenstein's suggestion was adopted. The original rendering was "there must be exactly as many things to distinguish".

4.062   Wittgenstein's suggestion was adopted.

4.112   Ogden had proposed "but that propositions become clear", but eventually printed "but to make propositions clear" which was Russell's translation in the Introduction.

4.12   The "the" was eventually omitted. Note that Wittgenstein says that it was Russell who had put in the "the". He could hardly have had this information from any other source than Ogden. There is no mark in the typescript which would clearly indicate which changes in it are Russell's. The handwriting and ink used in writing the "the", however, constitute some independent evidence that the insertion here was actually made by him. (See also the Editor's comment to 5.143 below, p. 42.)

4.1211   Wittgenstein's proposal was accepted.

4.122   Ogden printed "holding" as suggested by Wittgenstein.

4.123   The word-order was changed as suggested by Wittgenstein.

4.1252   On the use of the symbol E see below, p. 48.

4.126   The suggestion adopted was "numerical sign". This translation of "Merkmal" by "characteristic" is standard.

4.1272   Ogden followed Wittgenstein's instructions and printed "pseudo-concept" and "pseudo-propositions".

4.128   Ogden changed "special" to "pre-eminent".

4.28   Ogden followed Wittgenstein's suggestion and changed "falsity" to "falsehood" throughout.

4.411   The passage was originally translated as follows: "It is a priori probable that the importation of the elementary

	propositions . . .". Partly following Wittgenstein's suggestion Ogden first changed this to "It seems probable even at first sight that the bringing in of the elementary propositions . . .". In the proofs Ogden changed "bringing in" to "introduction".
4.442	Ogden printed "propositional sign".
4.464	The passage was printed in accordance with Wittgenstein's suggestion.
4.5	Wittgenstein had crossed out the first comment on this remark. "Things are combined in such and such a way" was changed to "Such and such is the case".
5.101	The symbols in question are those of material implication and negation. In the M.S., *i.e.* the typescript of the German text, "C" instead of " $\supset$ " had been used for implication and "/" instead of " $\sim$ " for negation. Ostwald printed the symbols from the typescript without changing them. The typescript of the English translation uses the same barbaric symbols.
5.12	The last three sentences of this comment Wittgenstein crossed out. Evidently he was able to answer the question himself before sending the comments to Ogden. The passage, incidentally, shows that the Engelmann typescript and the off-print of Ostwald's printing had not yet reached Wittgenstein when he was writing this comment.
5.1311	Cf. comment on *5.101* above.
5.1361	Pears and McGuinness in their later translation fell into the same error as those who drafted the first translation which was corrected by Wittgenstein himself.
5.143	The words "Russell's note" are slightly puzzling. In the typescript there are corrections in Ogden's and in Wittgenstein's handwriting and also in a third hand, which is presumably Russell's. The beginning of this remark was originally translated "The contradiction is that which is common to those propositions . . .". It seems that Ogden had first changed this to "A contradiction is an element common to those propositions . . ." and Russell then to "A contradiction is something shared by those propositions . . .". Wittgenstein's suggestions about omitting the article were followed in the printing.
5.252	Ogden printed "Only in this way".
5.42	Cf. comment on *5.101* above.
5.43	"von vornherein" was left untranslated.
5.451	The passage under discussion had originally been translated as follows: "If denial is introduced we must understand the same thing by it in propositions of the form " $\sim$ p" as in

propositions like "$\sim(p \lor q)$", "$(\exists x).\sim fx$" and others."
Wittgenstein deleted the words "the same thing by" which
gives to the sentence a different meaning. He also inserted a
"just" after "$\sim p$".

5.452   Ogden printed "has proved necessary".

5.453   Cf. comment on 4.128 above, p. 29.

5.461   Ogden printed "is of great importance".

5.473   The comment refers to the last line in the first paragraph of
5.473. Here Ogden did not accept Wittgenstein's suggestion
but wrote in the margin "Clear enough. Yours no improve-
ment". This comment by Ogden, incidentally, strongly
indicates that the typescript was returned to Wittgenstein.

5.4731 Ogden printed "illogically".

5.4733 The context had originally been translated "Frege says:
Every rightly constructed proposition . . ." and was printed
"Frege says: Every legitimately constructed proposition . . .".

5.5   It looks as though the last sentence "It is all right in the German text." had been added later. Cf. the Editor's comment on
5.12 above and 4.003 below.

5.513   In the original translation the second sentence of this remark
begins "The common element of all symbols . . .". It is
printed "What is common to all symbols . . ." as suggested by
Wittgenstein.

5.514   Wittgenstein's suggestion was adopted.

5.5261 The translation originally had "This shows itself in the
fact . . .".

5.535   Here, as in 4.1272, Ogden followed the suggestion.

4.003   The passage is printed "And so it is not to be wondered at
that the deepest problems are really *no* problems". The place of
this comment and the reference in it to a sentence in the
German original can be taken as an indication that Wittgenstein had by now received the German text which he evidently
had not yet at hand when he commented on 5.12. (Cf.
comment on 5.12 above.)

5.25   The "that" was deleted.

5.542   This remark was originally translated as follows: "It is however clear that "A believes, that p", "A thinks p", "A says p",
are of the form " 'p' says p": and the question is about not the
co-ordination of a fact and an object but with the co-ordination
of facts via co-ordination of their objects." It seems that
Ogden himself changed "It is however" to "But it is", but
that all the other changes in this passage are by Wittgenstein.

5.5423 The "together" was deleted.

5.552   The correction was made as in 4.023 and 4.5 above.

5.551   The translation originally was "And if we get into such a state that we need to answer". The printed version runs "And if we get into a situation where we need to answer..." as suggested by Wittgenstein.

5.553   *I.e.* "pre-eminent".

5.5542 The "not" was dropped.

5.61   Ogden printed "we cannot therefore *say* what we cannot think".

5.62   The passage had originally been translated "This note gives the key to deciding the question, in how far solipsism is a truth." Ogden did not react to Wittgenstein's suggestion. See comment on the same remark below, p. 50 and p. 53.

6   The translation originally was "The general form of the truth-function is:...". The second "the" was omitted according to Wittgenstein's instruction.

6.111   Ogden printed "... and this is a certain symptom of its being falsely understood."

6.121   "null-method" was changed to "zero-method". The change looks like Ramsey's hand.

6.2341 In the original translation this proposition began "Russell, Whitehead and Frege have not understood the essential of mathematical method, that is, working with equations." This corresponds to Wittgenstein's German typescript and to the Ostwald printing. For the 1922 printing Wittgenstein changed the German as indicated in his comment. The English version became "The essential of mathematical method is working with equations." It seems quite certain that Wittgenstein, when commenting on 6.2341 had with him the German original.

6.31   Wittgenstein's suggestion was followed and the original "And so it, too, is not a law a priori" changed to "And therefore it cannot be a law a priori either".

6.341   The proposition as printed begins "Whatever kind of picture these make I can ...".

6.342   Ogden accepted Wittgenstein's new wording of the passage but italicized the "*this*" and not, as Wittgenstein had wanted, the "*does*".

6.3431 The change suggested by Wittgenstein was accepted.

6.361   The printed text follows the original translation. "Only *uniform* connexions are *thinkable*."

6.362   Wittgenstein's suggestion was adopted. The translation originally ran "What can be described can also happen ..."

6.372   The passage had originally been translated "So people hold fast to natural laws as to something unassailable, . . .". What was printed goes "So people stop short at natural laws as at something unassailable, . . .".

6.41   Ogden followed Wittgenstein's suggestions.

6.43   The translation originally was "The world of the happy man is quite another than that of the unhappy". Following Wittgenstein's suggestion "man" was omitted.

6.4311   Wittgenstein's proposal was accepted.

6.4312   The passage under discussion was originally translated as follows: "The temporal immortality of the soul of man, that is to say its eternal survival also after death, is not only in no way guaranteed, but this assumption in the first place does not at all effect what men have always wished to attain by it." In the typescript Wittgenstein substituted for the end of the sentence the words ". . . first place will not do for us what one always would make it do." The final printing goes: ". . . first place will not do for us what we always tried to make it do." Ogden retained "riddle" in the translation.

6.4321   Ogden substituted "its performance" for "the solution".

6.44   "element" was dropped.

6.45   Following Wittgenstein's suggestion, Ogden changed "element" to "feeling".

6.52   Ogden followed Wittgenstein's suggestion and changed "are" to "be".

6.522   "element" was dropped.

0.3   [Trattenbach]
                                                          5.5.1922

Dear Ogden,

I am very sorry indeed I cannot send you the supplements.
There can be no thought of printing them. What they contain is
this: When I had finished the book *roughly* there remained certain
prop[osition]s – about a hundred – about which I was doubtful
whether I should take them in or not. These prop[osition]s
were – partly – different versions of those now contained in the
book; for it had often happened that I had written down a
prop[osition] in many different forms, when the same thought had
occurred to me in different ways during the long time I worked at
that business. Another part of the supplements are merely sketches
of prop[osition]s which I thought I might some day take up again
if their thoughts should ever revive in me. That means: The
supplements are exact⟨e⟩ly what must *not* be printed. Besides
they real[l]y contain no elucidations at all, but are
still less clear than the rest of my prop[osition]s. As to the
shortness of the book I am *awfully sorry for it; but what can I do*?!
If you were to squeeze me out like a lemon you would get
nothing more out of me. To let you print the Ergänzungen
would be no remedy. It would be just as if you had gone to a
joiner and ordered a table and he had made the table too short and
now would sell you the shavings and sawdust and other
rub[b]ish along with the table to make up for its shortness.
(Rather than print the Ergänzungen to make the book fatter
leave a dozen white sheets for the reader to swear into⟨o⟩ when
he has purchased the book and can⟨n⟩'t understand it.)

The title of the book must – I think – be printed twice: Once
in front of the whole book and then again before my preface
(as you suggested). Thus the succession would be:

Title (only English)
Russell's Introduction

Title (again)   ⎫(in the English as well as in the translation)
Dedication Motto   ⎬
Preface   ⎩This is the part I am responsible for and
No 1 etc.   therefore must be left together

I was very interested to hear that Johnson's book has appeared (I like Johnson *very* much.) And I should like to see his book. Perhaps it will be possible someday. – So don't be angry that I cannot make my book bigger. I would if I could.

Yours sincerely

L. Wittgenstein

supplements ("*Ergänzungen*"). – See above, p. 26, and the Editor's comments on p. 39f.

Succession of first pages. – The page following after Russell's Introduction has the Latin title, the dedication, and the motto. Above the German *Vorwort* is then printed the title in German, and above the English Preface the Latin title. The title is thus actually printed *three* times. The second occurrence of "English" in the letter is presumably a slip of the pen for "German".)

Johnson's book. – The first part of Johnson's *Logic* appeared in 1921 and the second in 1922. The third part was published in 1924. There is no evidence that Wittgenstein ever studied Johnson's *Logic*.

0.4   Trattenbach bei Kirchberg am Wechsel
                                       Nieder Österreich
                                       10.5.1922

DEAR OGDEN,

I hope you got my answer to your unregistered letter and I sup[p]ose you cursed me for not sending the Ergänzungen. By the way – printing my preface in German would make the book slightly big[g]er and would prevent people to think, that I had the cheek to write an English preface and moreover it would make the sense of the preface and the book plainer.

About quotation marks and italics do as you please.

F. P. Ramsey[']s first remark rather puzzles me. What I wrote is PRECISELY the same Ramsey means, only it's written in a slightly different notation WHICH HOWEVER IS QUITE A USUAL ONE. $\sum_{0}^{n} \nu$ means EXACTLY the same thing as $\sum_{\nu=0}^{\nu=n}$. I DIDN'T write $\sum_{0}^{n} \nu \cdot \binom{n}{\nu}$ but the ν should be printed a little smaller and then $\sum_{0}^{n} \nu$ simply means that the ν is to run through all the values from o to n. Exactly the same applies to the second formula where $\sum_{0}^{K_n} \varkappa$ means the same thing as $\sum_{\varkappa=0}^{\varkappa=K_n} \varkappa$. I wrote $\sum_{0}^{K_n} \varkappa \binom{K_n}{\varkappa}$,[1] and NOT $\sum_{0}^{K_n} \varkappa \cdot \binom{K_n}{\varkappa}$ what of course would be wrong. However to avoid misunderstandings you may just as well print the formulae in the way Ramsey wrote them.

His second remark about the E was true. *I had quite forgotten* that Russell uses $\exists$ where I wrote E. Therefore it ought to be $\exists$ always in my book. Please alter it if it's possible. Russell was merely conforming to my text.

Wherever I agreed with your translation I have put a + and if necessary have written a mark in the margin. To such points to which a longer remark is necessary I have put a −.

---

[1] Here Wittgenstein had inserted between the lines "This isn't a product of $\varkappa$ and $\binom{K_n}{\varkappa}$.

Remarks

Preface: "... if there were one person ...". This gives my meaning for I real[l]y meant one single by "Einem" but it sounds very odd in English and rather clumsy but if that can⟨n⟩'t be helped leave it as it is.

3.24   I wrote "symbolism" and not "symbol" for there isn't *one* symbol for generality but a whole complex e.g. in "($\exists$x).f(x)". But perhaps the word "notation" would be right. In fact I think it is. So the prop[osition] would become: "The notation for generality *contains* ..." or "The generality notation ..." but this I sup[p]ose would be bad English.

4.112   This seems to me wrong now. I think it cannot be the RESULT of philosophy "to make prop[osition]s clear": this can only be it⟨'⟩s TASK. The *result* must be that the prop[osition]s *now have become clear* that they ARE clear. Or can your translation be understood in this way also? If so, it's all right. If not rather leave "clarification". I sup[p]ose one can⟨n⟩'t say "the clearing up". Has this got a slightly different meaning?

4.27, 4.42   See above.

4.4611   If one cannot say "similarly as" one might perhaps say "... not however senseless; they are part of the symbolism in a way similar to that in which "O" $\left\{ \begin{array}{l} \text{is part of the} \\ \text{belongs to} \end{array} \right\}$ the symbolism of ...". If this is English please put it thus, or something of the same meaning.

5.523   Here I want to use *symbol* and not *symbolism* because I refer to the variable x or y etc. in ($\exists$x, y) ... and not to the whole complex of symbols as before. I own this is very dark but please leave "symbol" here and *don't* make it uniform with 3.24. Somebody may possibly understand me and if they don't never mind!

5.535   "... This solves all problems ...". *This isn't what I meant to say*! I said that all the problems which arise through

Russell[']s Axiom of Infinity *are to be* solved at this point. That is to say if a man wants to solve them, *this* is the point of the investigation where he must tackle them, for here they all lie *in nuce*. I propose "All the problems which arise $\begin{Bmatrix} \text{through} \\ \text{from} \end{Bmatrix}$ Russell's "Axiom of Infinity" ..." instead of "... is responsible for".

5.5563   "... logically completely ordered." By this I meant to say that the prop[osition]s of our ordinary language are not in any way logically *less correct* or less exact or *more confused* than prop[osition]s written down, say, in Russell[']s symbolism or any other "Begriffsschrift". (Only it is easier for us to gather their logical form when they are expressed in an appropriate symbolism.)

5.5563   As to "That most simple ..." I wanted to use the expression in the same way in which one talks of the "*highest good*" or "the good and the beautiful⟨l⟩". If however this is impossible in English leave "thing", al⟨l⟩though I don't like it a bit.

5.62   You made no remark to this prop[osition]. Couldn't one say "... provides $\begin{Bmatrix} \text{the} \\ \text{a} \end{Bmatrix}$ key to the decision of the question ..."? Or "By means of this remark we can decide the question ...". Perhaps this is better?

6.342   "in question" seems to me wrong. There seems to be a misunderstanding: By "as is indeed the case" I meant to say "in which indeed it is described". And one might put it thus "... that it can be described in that particular way in which indeed it is described." If "as is indeed the case" does not give this sense please alter it in the way I suggested or something like it.

6.3431   I think instead of "yet" I ought to have put "still" in a sense similar to that in which one might say: Al⟨l⟩though the wall is very thick *still* you hear his voice through it. "... the physical laws still speak of ..." would this do? (If not leave "still" out.)

6.54 *Here you misunderstand my meaning entirely.* I didn't mean to
use "elucidate" intransitive[ly]: what I meant to say was:
My prop[osition]s elucidate – whatever they do elucidate
– in this way: etc.

Similarly I might have said "My prop[osition]s clarify in
this way . . ." meaning "My prop[osition]s clarify whatever they do clarify – say, the prop[osition]s of natural
science – in this way: . . .". Here clarify is *not* used intransitive[ly] al⟨l⟩though the object is not mentioned.

You may put it thus: "My prop[osition]s elucidate philosophic matters in this way: . . .". This is something like
the right meaning. Or "My prop[osition]s are elucidations
in this way: . . ." but this I suppose is bad. If nothing
better is suggested and my first way of putting it real[l]y
won't do add "philosophic matters" as above.

I hope I have made myself plain.
Is Keynes still at Kings Coll[ege]. If so please remember
me to him.

Yours sincerely
LUDWIG WITTGENSTEIN

EDITOR'S COMMENTS

Ramsey's Remarks. – Ogden had evidently asked F. P. Ramsey to check the typescript of the English translation after Wittgenstein had returned it. The only comments of Ramsey's which have been preserved are the two "remarks" referred to in the letter.

The first remark refers to the formulae in 4.27 and 4.42. It seems that Ramsey had misunderstood the notation originally used by Wittgenstein. (The nature of the misunderstanding is indicated in the footnote on p. 48 above.) The formulae were eventually printed in the way suggested by Ramsey and approved of by Wittgenstein. The change in 4.27 is written in the margin of the typescript in Wittgenstein's hand. This indicates that the typescript was returned to Wittgenstein with Ogden's Questionnaire. The first remark is jotted down on two loose sheets of paper, evidently in Ramsey's hand. The second remark occurs on one of those sheets and is written by Ogden. It runs as follows:

"As to Russell's *Symbolism* Ramsey points out that E is always ∃ in brackets and only E when there is a shriek. I have written to Russell to query this as I see he has an E like you have in his introduction (but *he* may have been merely conforming to your text)."

Wittgenstein's suggestion that the E in the typescript be changed to ∃ was adopted for the printing.

The signs + and − refer to Wittgenstein's annotations on the Questionnaire which Wittgenstein had received from Ogden and which he returned with this letter. The Questionnaire is here reproduced as a facsimile. (Below, after p. 54.)

3.24   See Questionnaire. Ogden printed as suggested by Wittgenstein "(The notation for generality *contains* a prototype.)"

4.112   The passage in the remark under discussion had originally been translated 'The result of philosophy is not "philosophical propositions", but clarification of propositions'. Wittgenstein, when returning the typescript of the translation, added the words "a number of" after the "not". It was evidently Ogden's suggestion that "clarification of propositions" should be changed to "to make propositions clear". (Cf. Questionnaire.) The passage as printed reads 'The result of philosophy is not a number of "philosophical propositions", but to make propositions clear.' As seen from a note in the margin of the proofs, Ogden here opted for the way in which Russell had rendered this passage in his Introduction to the book. (Cf. *Tractatus*, the printed text, p. 11.)

4.27, 4.42 These remarks contain the formulae which Ramsey had wanted corrected.

4.4611 See Questionnaire. In the typescript Wittgenstein had changed "just as" to "similarly as".

5.523 The translation was originally "The generality designation occurs as argument." Wittgenstein inserted "an" after "as" and changed "designation" to "symbol". Before writing "symbol" however, he had written "symbolism". The final printing is "The generality symbol occurs as an argument."

5.535 As seen from the Questionnaire, Ogden followed Wittgenstein's suggestions. The translation had originally been 'All Problems which Russell's "Axiom of infinity" brings with it, are to be solved here.'

5.5563 "... logically completely ordered." was in fact the way the passage was originally translated. Ogden now suggested that "ordered" be changed to "in order". This is how the printed text goes and seems to accord with the meaning explanation given by Wittgenstein.

The printed text retains the word "thing" to which Wittgenstein had objected.

5.62 See above, p. 34, and Editor's comment. Here Ogden did not follow Wittgenstein's suggestions. The remark, as printed, runs: "This remark provides a key to the question, to what extent solipsism is a truth."

6.342 The translation of the passage referred to seems to have caused difficulties. Originally the translation ran: "So too the fact that it can be described by Newtonian mechanics asserts nothing about the world; or rather it asserts that it can be so described, as is indeed the case." When returning the typescript, Wittgenstein had changed the second half of the sentence to "; but *this* asserts something, namely, that it can be described in that particular way, as is indeed the case." Ogden's final version which was printed is "; but *this* asserts something, namely, that it can be described in that particular way in which it is described, as is indeed the case." It seems to the Editor that the version here suggested by Wittgenstein "; but *this* asserts something, namely, that it can be described in that particular way in which indeed it is described." is clearer.

6.3431 Wittgenstein's suggestion that "yet" be changed to "still" was adopted by Ogden.

6.54 The original translation of this passage had been "My propositions are explained in that he who understands me...". When returning the typescript Wittgenstein changed this to

"My propositions elucidate in this way that he who understands me . . .". As seen from the Questionnaire, Ogden suggested "My propositions are elucidated in this way; he who understands me . . .". Wittgenstein convinced Ogden that this was a misunderstanding and Ogden then changed "are elucidated" to "are elucidatory" and this is how the passage is printed.

The next eight pages contain a facsimile of a questionnaire sent by C. K. Ogden to Wittgenstein in May 1922, relating to specific points in the English translation of the *Tractatus*. Annotations in red are by Wittgenstein The large black ticks which appear on the margins of the facsimile are in blue crayon in the original typescript of the questionnaire. See above *0.4* and Editor's comments, pp. 48-54.

Preface.   Its object would be attained if there were one
             person who read it with understanding and to whom it
             afforded pleasure.

in stead of "afforded pleasure & one who reads it with understanding" as you corrected which is not good English if you mean one. Einem on a single one

2.1.   We make to ourselves pictures of facts.

This is the way free Russell's introduction goes instead of 'for'. It is a slightly old English term & quite suitable

2.1511.   Thus the picture is linked with reality; it reaches
            up to it.   *"Thus" is all right.*

You had put Such the picture in a connection for so linked. Such is impossible & I think you may have meant to change these words too & forgotten? Thus makes good English, or do you mean a forward reference?

3.24.   We **know** that everything is not yet determined by
            this proposition. (The symbol for generality **contains**
            a prototype.)

notation

See 5.22
   5.23

*You put 'symbolism' instead of 'symbolisation of'. This does not seem natural as English, and as we don't quite understand the point we suggest **symbol**, and or confirmation*

3.315   If we change a constituent part of a proposition into
            a variable, there is a class of propositions which are
            all the values of the resulting variable proposition.
            This class in general still depends on what, by arbi-
            trary agreement, we mean by parts of that proposition.
            But if we change all those signs/whose meaning was
            arbitrarily determined, into variables, there/always
            remains such a class.   But this is now no longer
            dependent on any agreement; ~~but~~ depends only on the
            nature of the proposition. It corresponds to a logical
            form, to a logical prototype.

omit comma

it

and

Still admitted. You have still j and above. There seem to be too many that; I suggest it Leave "it" or omit the that as just before suggested

3.317   And <u>only</u> this is essential to the determination, <u>that</u>
it is only a description of symbols and asserts nothing about
what is symbolised.

The way in which we describe the proposition is not
essential.

I think in suggested unessential. This reads naturally

3.322   It can never indicate the common characteristic of two
no comma objects that we symbolise them with the same signs, but by
different methods of symbolising. For the sign is arbitrary.
We could therefore equally well choose two different signs and
where then would be what was common in the symbolisation?

Jan said as well choose.   This is better if right
All right.

*this I think
is now
accurate*

3.325   In order to avoid these errors, we must employ a symbolism
which excludes them, by not applying the same sign in different symbols and by not applying signs in the same way which
signify in different ways.   A symbolism, that is to say, which
obeys the rules of <u>logical</u> grammar - of logical syntax.

*Leave out "externally"
Externally omitted here. It is very
obscure if put in. Is it wanted? & is it
the right word?*

4.023   The proposition determines reality to this extent, that
one only needs to say 'Yes' or 'No' to it to make it agree
*this
seems
the best* with reality.

The proposition constructs a world with the help of a
logical scaffolding, and therefore one can actually see in the
proposition all the logical features possessed by reality if
it is true.
One can draw conclusions from a false proposition.

I think this meets your requirement

4.112   The result of philosophy is not a number of "philosophical

propositions", but ~~to make~~ propositions ~~become~~ clear.

      Philosophy should make clear and delimit sharply the

thoughts which otherwise are, as it were, opaque and blurred.

4.27. *Symbol. (See Letter)*   *This is our mistake for clarifying idea*
4.4 . *Symbol. (See letter).*   *in the second place to which you objected*

4.4611   Tautology and contradiction are ~~not~~ however senseless;

they ~~belong to~~ *are part of* the symbolism, as "0" ~~belongs~~ to the symbolism

of Arithmetic.

you cannot say similarly as
as you cannot just as: as above
is absurd

4.462   In the tautology the conditions of agreement with the

~~(cancel?)~~ world - the presenting relations - *cancel* ~~cancel~~ one another, so that

it stands in no presenting relation to reality.

cancel is quite good
English but do you perhaps mean the
rather more the mathematical term Cancel

4.464   The truth of tautology is certain, of propositions possi-

ble, of contradiction impossible. (Certain, possible, impossible:

here we have ~~a suggestion~~ *an indication* of that gradation which we need in

the theory of probability).

I think "indication" is the right word
a symptom. as you write ?
(an indication!)

5.135   In no way can an inference be made from the existence of

one state of affairs to the existence of another entirely

different from it.

you had corrected schluss from
conclusion to inference above, so
I have put it here instead of
conclusion be drawn

5.1361   The events of the future cannot be inferred from those

of the present.

      Superstition is the belief in the causal nexus.

I have changed
this from "we
cannot infer"

and here I suffor inferred also
schlieren is rather than deduced

5.43   That from a fact p an infinite number of <u>others</u> should
follow namely $\sim\sim p, \sim\sim\sim\sim p$, etc., is indeed hardly to be believed
and it is not less wonderful that the infinite number of propositions of logic (of mathematics) should follow from half a dozen
"primitive propositions".

*you had put in <u>of</u>, which is not the English idiom
unless there is some special point "leave out of"*

5.454   In logic there cannot be (a) more general and a) more specia
*"a" is all right 'a more general' is quite natural a good English
and equals 'anything more general' which does not go well
you had tried all this & crossed it out leaving
a either*

5.473   ("Socrates is identical" means nothing because there is no
property which is called "identical". The proposition is senseless because we have not made some arbitrary determination, not
because the symbol is in itself unpermissible.)

In a certain sense we cannot make mistakes in logic.

*it does not now imply that
the symbol <u>is</u> unpermissible
with the out pointed this is now clear
enough and does not mislead as you feared*

5.522   That which is peculiar to the generality symbolism is
firstly, that it refers to a logical prototype, and secondly,
that it makes constants prominent.

*See 3.24 also Put "symbolism of generality" this is very awkward
you can say "symbolism of generality" or generality
symbol, or symbol for generality*

5.523   The generality symbol occurs as an argument.

*you seem to have made symbol by crossing
out that the is in here. This is alright, but
should be unanimous
with the then*

5.526   One can describe the world completely by completely
generalised propositions, i.e. without from the first co-ordina-
ting any name with a definite object

Put "outset".

*outset is better than first
or omit it if not
essential*

5.535 ~~This solves all problems for which~~ Russell's "Axiom of Infinity" is responsible.

What the Axiom of Infinity is meant to say would be expressed in language by the fact that there is an infinite number of names with different meanings.

5.5351 (It is nonsense to place the hypothesis p ⊃ p before a proposition in order to ensure that its arguments have the right form, because the hypothesis for a non-proposition as argument becomes not false but meaningless, and because the proposition itself becomes senseless for arguments of ~~an incorrect type~~ *of the wrong kind* and therefore it survives the wrong arguments no better and no worse than the senseless hypothesis attached for this purpose.)

5.5352 ~~Similarly,~~ one wanted to express "There are no things" by "~(∃x). x=x". But even if this were a proposition - would it not be true if indeed "There were things", but these were not identical with themselves?

5.541 At first sight it appears as if there were also a different way in which one proposition could occur in another.

'ordered' is very odd
is this right

5.5563 ~~———~~ All propositions of our colloquial language are actually,

just as they are, logically completely in order.— That

most simple thing which we ought to give here is not an image

of truth but the complete truth itself.

You have crossed out thing which leaves

the sentence meaningless like "The most ~~red~~ red which
we ought to eat is an apple." I expect you mean
to add other words

5.557   It is clear that logic may not collide with its application

This is right

You had put It is clear : Logic instead of That is clear : Lo
(Changing That to it) If you change the that
to it a ~~colon~~ stop is unnatural a another
that should fol

5.62   This remark provides a key to the question, ~~in~~ how far
to what extent

solipsism is a truth.

5.631   The thinking, presenting subject; ~~is~~ there is no such

thing.   Put ;———

You had a comma
only a ; or — is
better?

6.002   If we are given the general form of the way in which a

proposition is constructed, then thereby we are also given the

general form of the way in which by an operation out of one

proposition another can be created.

You cannot say of how

(We had by which) this is
unnatural

6.12   The fact that the proposition of logic are tautologies

shows the formal - logical - properties of language, of the

world.

You changed the sentence and left
it begins That
The English seems to require the fact
that, if this is right sense

6.1265 ✓ Logic can always be conceived to be such that every proposition is its own proof.

We have added to be
for explicit idiom

6.2341 ✦ The essential of mathematical method is/working with equations. On this method depends the fact that every proposition of mathematics must be self-intelligible.

You had put the working
and that is unnatural

6.342 ✓ So too the fact that it can be described by Newtonian mechanics asserts nothing about the world; but this asserts something, namely, that it can be described in ~~the~~ *that* particular way ~~that was adopted~~ *in which indeed it is described* ~~in question, as is indeed the case.~~

We have added in question if this is in accordance
with the meaning; the particular way is odd

6.3431 Through the whole apparatus of logic the physical laws *still* ⟋ speak of the objects of the world.

Would you like ?
"always"

I in have a yet
in here. It reads
oddly; one cannot
put it that

6.372 ✦ So people stop short at natural laws as at something unassailable, as did the ancients at God and Fate.

All right Does this get your meaning
It means they do not inquire further.
incorporate it if you think
unassailable better than
Is unapproachable
unassailable which
implies that they thought
they had a firm foundation
against enquiries.

6.4312   ✠ The temporal immortality of the soul of man, that is
            to say its eternal survival also after death, is not only
            in no way guaranteed, but this assumption in the first place
            will not do for us what we always tried to make it do.

            *I think, this best gets your
            meaning*

6.4321   ✠   The facts all belong only to the task and not to its
            performance.

            *This is the right word you wanted I think,
            (instead of wouldn't)*

6.51   ✠   Scepticism is not irrefutable, but palpably senseless,
            if it would doubt where a question cannot be asked.

            | This is idiomatic instead of will

            are elucidatory

─ 6.54   My propositions are elucidated in this way: he who
            understands me finally recognises them as senseless, when he
            has climbed out through them, on them, over them. (He must so
            to speak throw away the ladder, after he has climbed up on it.

            *you have not elucidate. The word
            will not stand an intransitive
            use = become clear
            (as one might say the
            itamin clarified "which
            is not good English nevertheless)*

0.5   23.6.1922

DEAR OGDEN,

Enclosed please find my declaration as you wanted it.

As to the complimentary copy I don't like the idea of your sending one to anybody at your expense; but I would like to get two or three copies of the book at my expense if I can possibly afford it (please let me know the price). If not I will perhaps ask Russell to lend me the money till I can pay him back.

If you will do me a favour however be so kind and try to find out Mrs Fan[n]y Pinsent's address in Birmingham. She is David Pinsent's mother to whom I dedicated the book *and I must send her a copy*. I hope very much you shall be able to find out where she lives and let me know. By the way: if I give to Messr[s]. Kegan Paul all publication rights then they ought to print my preface in German too!!! *For the preface is part of the book.*

If you see Johnson, Keynes or Bond please remember me to them. I wish I could hear⟨e⟩ of Johnson.

Yours sincerely

L. WITTGENSTEIN

Declaration. – This is dated Trattenbach 22nd June 1922 and reads as follows: "I hereby give to Messrs Kegan Paul all publication rights of my 'Logisch-Philosophische Abhandlung' in consideration of their issuing it in German and English in the 'International Library of Psychology and Philosophy' under the title *Tractatus logico-philosophicus*. Ludwig Wittgenstein." – The Memorandum of Agreement is between Kegan Paul, Trench, Trubner and Company Ltd. on the one part and C. K. Ogden on the other part. The date of the Agreement is 11th July 1922.

Complimentary copies. – See above, the Introduction, p. 11.

0.6 [Vienna]

17.7.1922

DEAR OGDEN,

Thanks for your letter dated 6.7. and all good news about the book. I've left Trattenbach now. My present address is: L.W. bei Frau Mima Sjögren. XIII. St. Veitgasse 17. Wien. This will al⟨l⟩ways find me. Letters to Trattenbach will be forwarded too. I should like to see Sprott and have a chat with him about the Cambridge people, and I should *very* much like to hear from Ritchie again after such a long time.

I hope to see Russell during the holiday⟨e⟩s.

Yours sincerely

LUDWIG WITTGENSTEIN

Sprott. – W. J. H. Sprott, b. 1897, then Demonstrator in the Psychological Laboratory at Cambridge, later Professor of Philosophy and of Psychology in Nottingham University.

Ritchie. – A. D. Ritchie (1891–1967), physiologist and philosopher, then Fellow of Trinity College, Cambridge, later Professor of Logic and Metaphysics at Edinburgh.

Russell. – See below, p. 58.

0.7 4.8.1922

DEAR OGDEN,

I am very sorry I could not send you the proofs before today. They were forwarded to me to Vienna and had to be sent to Hallein near Salzburg where I am staying just now with an uncle of mine. So they just arrived the day before yesterday.

I have looked through carefully all your notes and made my remarks where it was necessary. But as there was not sufficient room to explain myself in the margin I wrote them on a separate sheet which you will find enclosed.

I then read through *the whole of the German text* and of course found a good many faults which I corrected on the proof itself without mentioning them on a separate sheet. I hope the⟨e⟩se corrections are all of them intelligible. Several faults were made in separating syl[l]ables in German words when *one* half of the word stands on one line the other half on the next.

Now there was one difficulty in correcting the German: I haven't got my manuscript here. Therefore it often happened that I was not quite sure whether the text was right or wrong. *Now in such cases I put a sign such ← to the line in which I suspect a fault or about which I am not quite certain at any rate the arrow means*: "*please look up this line in the original and see if it's right*!" Especially it often happened that I was not sure about the *punctuation* [–] in this case I put a sign "P ←" before the line. So please compare the punctuation in these lines carefully with that of the original. Of course *the arrow doesn't mean that there is a fault but it just means that I'm not quite certain if there is or not*. In cases where I could easily explain my doubts I wrote some que⟨a⟩ries in the margin which – please – examine carefully.

As to your note about the Italian monastery etc. etc., do as you please; only I can⟨n⟩'t for my life see the point of it. Why should the general reviewer know my age? Is it as much as to say: You can⟨n⟩'t expect more of a young chap especially when he writes a book in such a noise as must have been on the Austrian front? If I knew that the general reviewer believed in astrology I would suggest to print the date and hour of my birth in front of the book that he might set *the horoscope* for me. (26/IV 1889. 6 p.m.)

I look forward very much to see Russell the day after tomorrow in Innsbruck. My address is as usual: L. W. bei Frau Mima Sjögren. XIII. St. Veitgasse 17, Wien.

Yours sincerely

LUDWIG WITTGENSTEIN

uncle. – Refers to Wittgenstein's uncle Paul. He seems to have been the only one of Wittgenstein's relatives who took an interest in his philosophical pursuits. In an early draft of a Preface for the "Logisch-philosophische Abhandlung" Wittgenstein expresses his thanks to his uncle for the encouragement he had given him.

my manuscript and *the original*. – By "my manuscript" Wittgenstein presumably meant the Engelmann typescript of the book (see above, p. 1). If this conjecture is right, "the original" can hardly mean anything but the off-print from Ostwald which Wittgenstein had corrected and returned to Ogden.

Italian monastery. – Evidently the famous monastery at Monte Cassino, the place where Wittgenstein was kept a prisoner of war until his release in August 1919.

Russell. – There is a reference to this meeting in Russell's *Autobiography* II, pp. 101.

COMMENTS II ON SEPARATE SHEETS

2.0123 If it isn't unenglish leave "know". It is used here in the sense in which one says "I know this man". If you *will* put "am acquainted" for it the prop[osition] must run thus: "If I am acquainted with an object, then I also know all its . . ." that means in the second occurrence there must be "know". "To know" means both: *kennen* and *wissen* and "to be acquainted with" – I think – hasn't exactly the meaning I want, because it seems to me to imply somehow that one knows a lot about an object, while to know here just means: I know *it* but I needn't know anything *about* it.

2.01231 As above: In the first occurrence you might put "be acquainted with", in the second leave "know".

2.02331 I don't think "without trouble" is good. I think the word "strai[gh]taway" has the right meaning. It would then run: ". . . one can distinguish it strai[gh]taway from the others by . . .".

2.06 Yes, this prop[osition] means "Reality is the existence and nonexistence of atomic facts". But couldn't we leave it as it is with "the"? I think it suits the preceding prop[osition] better. But do as you like about it.

2.181 Put "a".

3.203 If you put the full stop after "meaning" there must be one in the bracket too.

3.261 Put: "Nor any sign which . . .".

3.326 I think "significant" is al[l]right here. The meaning of this prop[osition] is: that in order to recognize the symbol in a sign we must look at how this sign is *used* significantly in propositions. I.e. we must observe how the sign is used in accordance with the laws of logical syntax. Thus "significant" here means as much as "syntactically correct".

3.331 No, this isn't meant imperatively. Put "into" for "to".

3.34   *Did I underline "welche allein" in the German. If so, it ought to be gesperrt.* If not, I don't know what was in my head when I underlined the English. If I didn't underline *the German* don't put italics in the English.

4.041   You might put "get outside it" instead of "get away from it".

4.0411 In the 3rd line leave out brackets in "Gen. fx". "Determine" *does* mean something like *discover* here. We can⟨n⟩'t distinguish between the two variables, we can⟨n⟩'t *find out* which is which.

4.0621 Couldn't the two "∼" in "(∼∼p=p)" be printed slightly nearer together? In the German they are a little nearer. They could al⟨l⟩ways be as close together as the "∼" is to "p". There needn't be a big[g]er space between "∼" and "∼" than between "∼" and "p".

4.112   If "to make" is better, please put it in. The whole, of course, is a Zeugma and there ought to be a substantive after "but" to match with "a number of...". But I suppose that can⟨n⟩'t be done.

4.1273 See proof: "aRb", "(∃x) : aRx.xRb", "(∃x,y) : aRx.xRy. yRb" are quite separate symbols they must therefore be slightly further apart from one another.

4.4   Omit "the".

4.465   "essence" is al[l]right.

4.466   leave "symbols".

5.02   It real[l]y ought to be "+_c" not "+c". "c" is a suffix.

5.101   Put: "p.∼q : ∨ : q.∼p".
        In the first line of the schema there should be square brackets round p⊃p.q⊃q. It doesn't matter that they are not square in the German. In the last line of the schema the round brackets want closing and there must be a bigger space between them and the square ones, just as in the top line. In the bottom line in the German please put "(p.∼p.q.∼q)" instead of "(p.∼p.∼q.q)".

5.1361 Don't print "Superstition" in italics! But leave the German "Aberglaube" gesperrt.

5.1362　"known" is al[l]right here.

5.155　Put "unit". Oughtn't there to be a *colon* in the first line in this prop[osition] before the capital "The" at the end of the line as in the German before "Die Umstände"?

5.3　Omit "the".

5.42　The last part of this prop[osition] ought to run: "And it is obvious that the "⊃" which we define by means of "∼" and "∨" is identical with that by which we define "∨" with the help of "∼" and that this "∨" is the same as the first, and so on." Thus your correction in the German is quite right only in the last case there ought to be "∨" instead of "∼" in the German and in the English.

5.473　*I believe it ought to be "some" here.* One might say in a similar sense: "the prop[osition] is senseless because *there is* SOME arbitrary determination which we have not made". I hope you can leave it as it is.

5.511　I suppose it should be "connected *into*". *I didn't mean* "connected with" *but*: connected to one another in such a way as to form an infinitely fine network. Could one say "I connect these bits of string into a network" meaning, I connect them in such a way as to form a network?

5.521　I mean "separate" and *not* "derive". They were connected and I separate them.

5.5261　"(∃x, φ) etc" not "(∃x.φ) etc".
　　　　The bracket should stand at the end of the prop[osition]. Put "A characteristic of a composite symbol . . ." as you suggested.

5.5303　Yes, this s⟨c⟩hould be "Roughly speaking:".

5.532　In the German it should be ". . .; und nicht . . .".

5.5563　"image" has the meaning of "simile" here. So you *may* put "simile".

6.121　"into" is right.

6.36111　The figure s⟨c⟩hould be thus

I.e. the little cross and the circle should be just at the end of each line and not at a distance from it [×⟋——⟍o] and they should be quite small; for they should just mark that the two ends of each line are different.

4.1272   Look at my correction. *Here the commas and quotation marks are printed wrongly*! It mustn't be »"Complex," "Fact," etc. etc.« *but*: »"Complex", "Fact", "Function", "Number", etc.« Similar nonsense you find above in the same prop[osition]: And in the German too. Please note this point when you look through the stuff again.

4.1273   In the 8th line from the top of this prop[osition]: Is there a comma wanted after "series", and ought it to be between the word and the quotation marks?

4.24   In the German exactly as in the English:
»"fx". "$\phi(x,y)$", etc.« in the English
»"fx", "$\phi(x,y)$", etc.« in the German

4.241   I wonder what has got into the printers head!

4.1252   The same faults. *In the German it is al[l]right.*

4.0411   „   „   „

4.441   „   „   „

4.442   „   „   „   If possible don't separate (TTFT) from (p,q) they ought to stand on the same line. The space between them should not be big[g]er than it is in the German.

5.02   The same fault. (First line.)
There is a fault in the translation of this prop[osition] caused perhaps by a misprint in the German. It must not be: "The index is always part of a description of the object whose names we attach to it . . ." *but*: ". . . of the object *to whose name we attach it* . . .". We don't attach the names of the object to the index but the index to the *name* of the object!

5.242   „, „   „ „,
wrong   right

5.31   The same fault

5.2523   „   „   „   5.534

5.42	,,	,,	,,	5.535
5.44	,,	,,	,,	5.5352
5.451	,,	,,	,,	5.541
5.46	,,	,,	,,	5.542
5.47	,,	,,	,,	5.631
5.473	,,	,,	,,	5.641
5.501	,,	,,	,,	6.1201
5.502	,,	,,	,,	6.1203
5.512	,,	,,	,,	6.1221
5.513	,,	,,	,,	6.1232
5.515	,,	,,	,,	6.36
5.525	,,	,,	,,	3.312
5.5301	,,	,,	,,	3.333
5.531	,,	,,	,,	
5.532	,,	,,	,,	

5.512   In the 5th line from the top "p" is left out after "∼".
It should be: "That which denies in "∼p"...".

5.5321   In this prop[osition] – I am afraid – something must be
altered (it is *my* fault). Instead of what I have crossed out
it must be: "(∃x).fx.⊃.fa : ∼(∃x,y).fx.fy".

2.0123   Ogden had queried the "know" and written in the margin 'Do you think we ought to have "am acquainted with" here?'

2.01231   Ogden had queried the two occurrences of "know" in this remark, but did *not* change either occurrence to "be acquainted with".

2.02331   The translation originally had "directly". Ogden suggested "without trouble", but adopted Wittgenstein's counter-proposal and printed "straight away". Ogden also made a few other changes in the typescript translation which Wittgenstein accepted.

2.06   Ogden had queried the last "the" in "The existence and non-existence of atomic facts is the reality" but left it in, following Wittgenstein's suggestion. Interestingly, Ogden's query made reference to 5.1361 where the word "Superstition" without article stood for the German "Der Aberglaube".

2.181   The translation originally had "the logical picture". This was changed to "a logical picture".

3.261   The last sentence of this remark was originally translated "Names *cannot* be taken to pieces by definition (No sign which alone and independently has a meaning)." Ogden suggested that "No sign" be changed either to "Nor any sign which" or "No sign, that is, which". In the proofs Ogden changed "definition" to the plural "definitions", inserted a full stop after that, and changed the first word in the brackets from "no" to "No". This corresponds best to the German text.

3.326   The printed version agrees with the original translation. But in the proofs Ogden had queried the phrase "the significant use" and suggested as a possible substitute "its symbolic use."

3.331   This is a reply to Ogden's note in the margin of the proofs: 'We suppose you do not mean "sehen wir hinüber" as imperative? "Let us turn to Russell's etc.". If the above is right *into* or *of* is perhaps better than the *to* after "view".' – The proofs and the original translation had "to" here.

3.34   In the printed text there are no italics, nor is the corresponding German *gesperrt*. It is the same with the Ostwald printing.

4.041   The translation originally had "get away from it". Ogden queried this in the proofs and suggested tentatively "get outside", of which Wittgenstein approved.

4.0411 Ogden had written in the margin of the proofs "'determine' looks as though it might mean *discover*".

4.112 Cf. comment on p. 28 above. "Zeugma" is used in German as a grammarian's term for the sort of asymmetry or incongruence exemplified in the English translation of 4.112. In the German sentence there is no "Zeugma"; the words "philosophische Sätze" answer symmetrically to "das Klarwerden von Sätzen".

4.465 The translation originally had "essential". The correction was by Ogden.

4.466 Ogden had questioned whether it should not be "combinations of signs" rather than "combinations of symbols".

5.155 The translation originally had "unity" (*sc.* of the probability proposition). The colon was put in.

5.42 In the Ostwald printing this remark contained a mistake which seems to have escaped Wittgenstein's notice until Ogden corrected it.

5.473 The translation originally had "an arbitrary determination". Wittgenstein changed "an" to "some" in the typescript; Ogden queried in the margin of the proofs whether it should not be "an" after all, but agreed to Wittgenstein's directive.

5.511 Wittgenstein is here agreeing to Ogden's suggestion that "to" be changed to "into".

5.521 The passage under discussion runs: "I separate the concept *all* from the truth-function." Ogden had queried whether "separate" should not be changed to "derive".

5.5261 Ogden suggested that "A characteristic of composite symbols" be changed to "A characteristic of a composite symbol". Wittgenstein agreed and this is how it was printed. The change is not marked in the proofs however. This would indicate that the final printing took place from another set of proofs into which Ogden inserted all the final corrections. This set of proofs has not been preserved. (See above, p. 11f.)

5.5303 The translation of the German "Beiläufig gesprochen" here, as in 2.0232, was originally "In parenthesis". Wittgenstein had changed the words in 2.0232 in the typescript to "Roughly speaking". Ogden now asks whether the same change ought not to be made in 5.5303 too and Wittgenstein answers in the affirmative.

5.5563 The original translation had been "image of truth" and Ogden's suggestion, to which Wittgenstein agreed was that "image" be changed to "simile".

4.1273 The comma was removed in the final printing, but there is no instruction to this effect in the proofs. This is another one of the many places which would indicate that the final printing was from a different set of proofs than the one which Wittgenstein returned to Ogden.

4.241 and the following. The faults of which Wittgenstein is complaining are the printer's habit of printing a comma or full stop before the end-quotation marks instead of in the reverse order. Thus, for example, in 4.241 "a," instead of "a",.

5.02 "First line" means first line in the second paragraph of this remark.

5.5321 The formula which Wittgenstein is here correcting in the German and the English proofs was originally "fa : ∼ (∃x,y).fx.fy". *This* formula occurs in the printing by Ostwald.

0.8   [Hasbach]
                                                         18.9.1922

DEAR OGDEN,

I have now got another post as school teacher. My address is: Hasbach bei Neunkirchen. Nieder Österreich.

I am very anxious to know how the book is going on. I hope no further difficulties have turned up during the printing.

Could you get Mrs. Pinsent[']s address? *Please let me know it, and all about the book* too. – This place is rather nice as far as nature goes but the people are as hideous as in Trattenbach.

Please remember me to Keynes if you see him and tell him he might right [write] me a line if he isn't too busy.

                          Yours very sincerely

                                  LUDWIG WITTGENSTEIN

0.9   [Puchberg]
                                                                   15.11.1922

DEAR OGDEN,

   Thanks so much for your letter and the books which arrived yesterday. They real[l]y look nice. I wish their contents were half as good as their external ap[p]earance.

   I'm af⟨f⟩raid there is no hope that you will ever be repaid in any way for the lots of trouble you took with my stuff.

   I hope you will get Mrs. Pinsent's address from Ri[t]chie. Otherwise, c⟨o⟩urse him from me.

   I'm sure Johnson won't buy my book. Though I should like to know what *he* thinks about it. If you see him please give him my love.

   I hope to hear from you again before too long.

                              Yours sincerely

                                    LUDWIG WITTGENSTEIN

P.S. My address has changed again; it is now: L. W. Lehrer in Puchberg am Schneeberg. Nieder Österreich.

0.10   [Puchberg]
                                          [March 1923]

DEAR OGDEN,

I have just got your P.C. dated March 17. "The meaning of
meaning" reached me a few days ago. The "other things" you
mention must have got lost, except Keynes's edition of the
Manchester Guardian. In the last month I have not been quite
well, my nerves being run down badly by much work and
excitement. This is the reason why I have not yet been able to
read your book thoroughly. I have however read in it and I think
I ought to confess to you frankly that I believe you have not quite
caught the problems which – for instance – I was at in my book
(whether or not I have given the correct solution). – My present
address is precisely the one you wrote to:

Puchberg am Schneeberg. Nieder-Österreich.

I should love to hear from Ritchie.

Please excuse my remark about your book. I did not make it
because I thought that you were interested in my opinion about
it, but me⟨a⟩rely for the sake of frankness.

I hope you can read this letter. I'm sure there are more faults
in it than words.

                          Yours sincerely
                          L. WITTGENSTEIN

The Meaning of Meaning: *a Study of the Influence of Language upon
Thought.* By C. K. Ogden and I. A. Richards. The International Library of
Psychology, Philosophy and Scientific Method. Kegan Paul, Trench,
Trubner & Co., Ltd. London 1923.

Keynes's edition. – This probably refers to Keynes's "Reconstruction
in Europe" which had been issued as a special supplement to the
Manchester Guardian.

0.11   [Puchberg]
                                                           27.3.1923

DEAR OGDEN,

I wrote to you the other day as an answer to your P.C. addressed
to Puchberg. Just now I got the card forwarded from Hasbach. I
got The Meaning of Meaning and the M. Guardian. I have *not*
heard from Keynes and haven't got the Times you mention. My
address is: Puchberg am Schneeberg Nieder-Österreich, Austria.

                              Fröhliche Ostern!

                                        Yours sincerely

                                        L. WITTGENSTEIN

Did Keynes write to me? If so, please tell him it hasn't reached me.

0.12   [Cambridge]
                                                [Spring 1929]

DEAR OGDEN,

Thanks so much for your kind intervention in my business with Messrs. Kegan Paul. The reason why I wanted my book is that I had to submit it as a dissertation for the Ph.D. and as this is not going to happen again I will never again want a free copy. In fact even now I wouldn't have complained but that I'm *very* short of money.

> Yours very sincerely
>
> L. WITTGENSTEIN

Wittgenstein received his degree in June 1929.

0.13

Sorry I cannot come to you today. Could you come and have tea with me some day next week? (Say Tuesday.)

L. WITTGENSTEIN

This short note was probably written some time after Wittgenstein's return to Cambridge in 1929.

0.14   Trinity College
                                              Cambridge
                                              21.6.33

DEAR OGDEN,

On May the 20th I got a letter from Kegan Paul saying that the first edition of my book was now nearly exhausted and that they were about to print a new one. They mentioned in their letter certain corrections which Ramsey had made and I had authorised and asked whether I wished to make any further alterations. I replied on May 27th that I did not know what Ramsey[']s corrections were and that I wanted to see them before the new edition went into print. I then did not hear from Kegan Paul until today when they write to me, would I "be good enough to return to them the corrected proofs of Tractatus L-Ph . . . these are now required urgently". Now this obviously makes no sense as they haven't sent me any proofs and some feeling warns me that they want to play a trick on me. So would you be so good to step in and help clear up this matter.

                         Yours sincerely

                              LUDWIG WITTGENSTEIN

A draft of Wittgenstein's reply of 27th May to the publishers has been preserved. In his letter Wittgenstein also raised the question of the publishers paying him a royalty on the new edition of the book. The publishers did not respond to Wittgenstein's suggestion. This offended Wittgenstein and was one reason why he did not wish his later works to be published by his first publishers.

On 27th June the publishers wrote to C. K. Ogden saying that Wittgenstein had returned the proofs with "a fair number of additional corrections himself". This would indicate that Wittgenstein had seen and checked proofs of the book in the time between 21st and 27th June.

Ramsey's corrections. – This phrase must refer to corrections made in the course of discussions which F. P. Ramsey had with Wittgenstein in Austria in 1923. (See the Appendix below.) The corrections were originally made in Ramsey's copy of the book. This copy still exists. A few years ago, Dr Casimir Lewy made a detailed study of these corrections and published his findings in a note in *Mind*. (C. Lewy, "A

Note on the Text of the *Tractatus*". *Mind 76*, 1967, pp. 416–423.) The corrections, incidentally, are mostly in Wittgenstein's handwriting. Most, but not all of them, were incorporated in the 1933 reprint. According to Lewy's study, there are only four significant changes in the 1933 reprint which are not marked in Ramsey's copy. These corrections could be the ones to which the Publishers referred in their letter to Ogden and of which they said there was "a fair number".

APPENDIX

Letters by F. P. Ramsey

1923–1924

SOME time in 1923 Wittgenstein got word from Ogden that Frank Ramsey would be coming to Austria. Wittgenstein then wrote to Ramsey with whom he had had no previous contact. An undated draft of the beginning of Wittgenstein's letter has been preserved. It goes as follows:

DEAR MR. RAMSEY,
I've got a letter from Mr. Ogden the other day saying that you may possibly come to Vienna in one of these next months. Now as you have so excellently translated the Tractatus into English I've no doubt you will be able to translate a letter too and therefore I'm going to write the rest of this one in German.

The German part of the letter has not been preserved. But eight letters or brief communications from Ramsey to Wittgenstein still exist. They are all from the years 1923 and 1924 when Ramsey visited Wittgenstein in Austria. (A single letter from Wittgenstein to Ramsey is known to exist; it dates from the year 1929.)

In 1923 Wittgenstein was a schoolmaster at Puchberg, a village in Lower Austria at the foot of the Schneeberg. (Cf. above, p. 12.) Ramsey came to see him here in September and stayed for a couple of weeks. During that time they spent several hours each day reading the *Tractatus*, with Wittgenstein explaining his thoughts to Ramsey. In the course of these discussions Wittgenstein also made numerous changes and corrections in the English translation and some in the German text. They were all written down in Ramsey's copy of the book, where they can still be studied. (See above p. 13.)

Ramsey has given a vivid account of his encounter with Wittgenstein in two letters which are preserved. The one was to John Maynard Keynes, the other to Ramsey's mother. The relevant passages from the letter to his mother, dated Puchberg am Schneeberg, 20th September 1923 read as follows:

Wittgenstein is a teacher in the Village school. He is very poor, at least he lives very economically. He has one *tiny* room whitewashed,

77

containing a bed, washstand, small table and one hard chair and that is
all there is room for. His evening meal which I shared last night is
rather unpleasant coarse bread butter and cocoa. His school hours are
8 to 12 or 1 and he seems to be free all the afternoon.

He looks younger than he can possibly be; but he says he has bad eyes
and a cold. But his general appearance is athletic. In explaining his
philosophy he is excited and makes vigorous gestures but relieves the
tension by a charming laugh. He has blue eyes.

He is prepared to give 4 or 5 hours a day to explaining his book. I
have had two days and got through 7 (+ incidental forward references)
out of 80 pages. And when the book is done I shall try to pump him for
ideas for its further development which I shall attempt. He says he
himself will do nothing more, not because he is bored, but because his
mind is no longer flexible. He says no one can do more than 5 or 10
years work at philosophy. (His book took 7.) And he is sure Russell
will do nothing more important. His idea of his book is not that
anyone by reading it will understand his ideas, but that some day
someone will think them out again for himself, and will derive great
pleasure from finding in this book their exact expressions. I think he
exaggerates his own verbal inspiration, it is much more careful than I
supposed but I think it reflects the way the ideas came to him which
might not be the same with another man.

He has already answered my chief difficulty which I have puzzled
over for a year and given up in despair myself and decided he had not
seen. (It is not in the 1st 7 pages but arose by the way.) He is great. I
used to think Moore a great man but beside W!

He says I shall forget everything he explains in a few days; Moore
in Norway said he understood W completely and when he got back to
England was no wiser than when he started.

It's terrible when he says "Is that clear" and I say "no" and he says
"Damn it's *horrid* to go through that again". Sometimes he says I can't
see that now we must leave it. He often forgot the meaning of what he
wrote within 5 min[ute]s, and then remembered it later. Some of his
sentences are intentionally ambiguous having an ordinary meaning and
a more difficult meaning which he also believes.

He is, I can see, a little annoyed that Russell is doing a new edit[ion]
of Principia because he thought he had shown R that it was so wrong
that a new edition would be futile. It must be done altogether afresh.
He had a week with Russell 4 y[ea]rs ago.[1]

---

[1] Refers to the meeting with Russell in The Hague in December 1919.
(See above, p. 10.)

Ramsey also sent a postcard to Ogden:

L. W. explains his book to me from 2–7 every day. It is most illuminating; he seems to enjoy this and as we get on about a page an hour I shall probably stay here a fortnight or more. He is very interested in it, though he says that his mind is no longer flexible and he can never write another book. He teaches in the village school from 8 to 12 or 1. He is very poor and seems to lead a very dreary life having only one friend here,[1] and being regarded by most of his colleagues as a little mad.

F.P.R.

In the course of Michaelmas and Lent Terms of the academic year 1923–1924 Ramsey wrote four longish letters to Wittgenstein. He speaks in them also about his own work and doings and of his (and Keynes's) efforts to induce Wittgenstein to visit Cambridge. From the second letter we further get the interesting information that Wittgenstein had evidently discussed with Ramsey the possibility of obtaining a Cambridge degree. He seems to have thought of somehow completing his studies for the B.A. degree which he had begun before the war. Ramsey told him this was no longer possible, but that Wittgenstein might obtain a Ph.D., if he came to Cambridge for another year and submitted a thesis. Eventually, Wittgenstein submitted the *Tractatus* as a thesis for the Ph.D. degree after his return to Cambridge in 1929. (See above, p. 12.)

Trinity
15 October 1923

DEAR WITTGENSTEIN,

I had a letter the other day from the waiter in the hotel at Puchberg, containing a bill I had not paid. (It was hardly my fault as the proprietor's son assured me I had paid everything). I sent him a cheque, but I'm afraid he may have some difficulty in cashing it. Would you be so good as to see if it is all right, and if not, let me know and explain the difficulty so that I can solve it if possible by some other method of payment? I'm sorry to trouble you but I don't think it will be much trouble as my cheque ought to do, if he waits till the bank has sent it over here.

[1] Rudolf Koder, then schoolteacher at Puchberg, life-long friend of Wittgenstein's.

I haven't seen Keynes yet to ask him about your degree.

I went to Salome at the Opera in Vienna; it was most beautifully staged and I entirely agree about the Opera House.[1] I stayed in Vienna 3 days and enjoyed myself looking at pictures and buildings.

I haven't started work on numbers yet as I have been busy preparing stuff to teach my women pupils. They pretend to understand more than I expected; but whether they do really, I don't know.

I am sending you my other copy of Tractatus at the same time as this letter.

Russell and his wife have just produced a book on "The Prospects of Industrial Civilisation" and he alone one called "The A.B.C. of the Atom"!

I have been talking to a man who knows Baron von Schrenck Notzing; he had seen the materialisation happening and taken photographs of it which he showed to me; they were astonishing. He is very smart and has detected a lot of very clever frauds but he is sure these things are genuine.

I am afraid the fare from Vienna to London is rather more than I thought. My ticket was K1,940,000.

I haven't yet found myself out in having forgotten anything you explained to me.

Yours ever

FRANK RAMSEY

Trinity
12 November 1923

DEAR WITTGENSTEIN,
   Thanks for your letter.

I have good news for you. If you will pay a visit to England, there is £50 (=K16,000,000) available to pay your expenses. So do, please, come. I imagine you would prefer to come in your summer holiday, which I think you said was July and August. The disadvantage of that time is that it is vacation in Cambridge, and the time when people in England take their holidays, so that the people you would like to see might be scattered all over the place. It occurred to me that if, as you said was possible, you were leaving your present school at the end of the academic year, you might perhaps leave two months earlier, and come to England for May and June, or longer, or part of those months. The Cambridge summer term is April 22nd to June 13th.

---

[1] A work of architecture of which Wittgenstein had a high opinion. Ed.

I asked Keynes about your degree, and the position seems to be this. The regulations have changed so that it is no longer possible to obtain a B.A. by keeping six terms and submitting a thesis. Instead you can obtain a Ph.D by 3 years and a thesis. If you could come here for another year, you could probably get permission to count your two previous years and so obtain a Ph.D. But that is the only possibility.

I have not been doing much towards reconstructing mathematics; partly because I have been reading miscellaneous things, a little Relativity and a little Kant, and Frege. I do agree that Frege is wonderful; I enjoyed his critique of the theory of irrationals in the Grundgesetze enormously. I should like to read Ueber die Zahlen des Herrn H. Schubert but haven't yet found a copy only this wonderful advertisement which I'm sure you would like to read again.

"Der Verfasser knüpft seine Betrachtungen an die Darstellung, die Herr Schubert in der Encyklopädie der mathematischen Wissenschaften von den Grundlagen der Arithmetik gegeben hat. Er entdeckt darin eine Methode und ein Prinzip, die vielleicht schon früher von anderen Forschern benutzt, aber, wie es scheint, noch nie als solche besonders in Auge gefasst und ausgesprochen worden sind; die Methode, störende Eigenschaften durch Absehen von ihnen zum Verschwinden zu bringen, und das Prinzip der Nichtunterscheidung des Verschiedenen, wie der Verfasser es nennt, das mit sehr interessanten histrionalen Eigenschaften der Zahlen enge zusammenzuhängen scheint. Indem der Verfasser das Wesen dieser Methode und dieses Prinzips genau in Worte auszusprechen und ihre Tragweite in helles Licht zu setzen sucht, glaubt er den Weg für weiter unabsehbare Fortschritte gebahnt zu haben."[1]

But I am awfully idle; and most of my energy has been absorbed since January by an unhappy passion for a married woman, which produced such psychological disorder, that I nearly resorted to psychoanalysis, and should probably have gone at Christmas to live

---

[1] *Tr. English*: The considerations of the author set out from the account of the foundations of arithmetic which Mr Schubert has given in the Encyclopaedia of the Mathematical Sciences. The author discovers there a method and a principle which perhaps have been used earlier by other investigators but, it seems, have never before been expressly studied and fully spelt out. This is the method of making distressing properties disappear by ignoring them and the principle of not distinguishing the different, as the author calls it, which appears intimately to be connected with interesting histrionic properties of numbers. By trying to give the essence of this method and this principle a precise formulation in words and to shed clear light on their relevance, he thinks he has paved the way for further unfathomable progress.

in Vienna for 9 months and be analysed, had not I suddenly got better a fortnight ago, since when I have been happy and done a fair amount of work.

I think I have solved all problems about finite integers, except such as are connected with the axiom of infinity, but I may well be wrong. But it seems to me too difficult to discuss by post, except that perhaps when I get an account of it written out I will send it to you. I wish you were here; do come in the Summer. Have you noticed the difficulty in expressing without = what Russell expresses by $(\exists x) : fx . x = a$?

I am reading The Brothers Karamazov, I think the scene described by Ivan between Christ and the Inquisitor is magnificent.

Yours ever
F. P. RAMSEY

Has Ogden sent you *my review of Tractatus in Mind*? if not, and you would like it I will send it to you, but it is not at all good and you must remember I wrote it before coming to see you.

20 December 1923

DEAR WITTGENSTEIN,

Thanks for your letter; I'm sorry you have been ill and depressed.

First, *the £50 belong to Keynes*. He asked me not to say so straight away because he was afraid you might be less likely to take it from him than from an unknown source, as he has never written to you. I can't understand why he hasn't written, nor can he explain, he says he must have some "complex" about it. He *speaks of you with warm affection and very much wants to see you again*. And also, apart from that, if you would like to come to England he would not like you to be unable to for want of money, of which he has plenty.

I quite understand your fear of not being fit for society, but you musn't give it much weight. I could get lodgings in Cambridge and you need not see more of people than you like or feel able to. I can see that staying with people might be difficult as you would inevitably be with them such a lot, *but if you lived by yourself you could come into society gradually*.

I don't want you to take this as endorsing your fear of boring or annoying people, for I know *I myself want to see you awfully*, but I just want to say that if you have such a fear surely it would be all right if you were not staying with anyone but lived alone at first.

I don't know how long you could live here on the £50, but I am sure it would be long enough to make it worth while for you to come.

I think Frege is more read now; two great mathematicians *Hilbert and Weyl* have been writing on the *foundations of mathematics* and *pay compliments to Frege*, appear in fact to have appreciated him to some extent. His unpopularity would naturally go as the generation he criticised dies.

I was silly to think I had solved those problems. I'm always doing that and finding it a mare's nest. (Moore does the same.) I will write to you about it soon at length, but I am afraid you will think my difficulties silly. I didn't think there was a real difficulty about $\exists x : fx . x = a$ ie that it was *an objection to your theory of identity*, but I didn't see how to express it, because I was under the silly delusion that if an x and an a occurred in the same proposition the x could not take the value a. I had also a reason for wanting it not to be possible to express it. But I will try to explain it all in about a fortnight from now, because it ought to help me to get clearer about things, and you may be able to put me right and may be interested. If I had anything of importance to say you would, I know, be interested, but I don't think I have.

I have been trying a lot to prove a proposition in the Mengenlehre either $2^{\aleph_0} = \aleph_1$, or $2^{\aleph_0} \neq \aleph_1$, which it is no one knows but I have had no success.

I made the acquaintance of your nephew Stonborough, whom I like.

I hear Russell is going to America to lecture.

I do hope you are better and no longer depressed and exhausted and will come to England.

Yours ever

FRANK RAMSEY

Thanks for giving me the expression $fa . \supset .(\exists x,y) . fx . fy : \sim fa \supset (\exists x)fx$.[1]

Trinity
20 February 1924

MY DEAR WITTGENSTEIN,

Thanks for your letter; except that I think you might enjoy it, *I* no longer want you to come here *this summer*, because *I am coming to Vienna*, for some and perhaps the whole of it! I can't say exactly when or for how long, but very likely, next month, so I shall hope to see you quite soon now.

This is for various reasons: I hope to settle permanently in Cambridge, but as I have always lived here, I want to go away for a time

---

[1]The handwriting is not clear and the Editor is therefore not quite sure whether he has reconstructed the formula correctly.

first, and have the chance now for six months. And if I live in Vienna I can learn German, and come and see you often, (unless you object) and *discuss my work with you*, which would be most helpful. Also I *have been very depressed* and done little work, and have *symptoms so closely resembling some of those described by Freud* that I shall probably *try to be psychoanalysed, for which Vienna would be very convenient*, and which would make me stay there the whole six months. *But I'm afraid you won't agree with this.*

Keynes still means to write to you; it really is a disease – his procrastination; but he doesn't (unlike me) take such disabilities so seriously as to go to Freud! He very much hopes you will come and see him.

I haven't seen *Johnson* for a long time but I am going to tea with his sister soon, and unless he is ill I will give him your love (last time I went there he was ill). *The third part of his Logic is to be published soon.* It deals with Causation.

I am so sorry you *are using up all your strength* struggling with your surroundings; *it must be terribly difficult with the other teachers.* Are you staying on in Puchberg? When I saw you, you *had some idea of leaving if it got too impossible, and becoming a gardener.*

I can't write about work, it is such an effort when my ideas are so vague, and I'm going to see you soon. Anyhow (?) I have done little except, I think, made out the proper solution rather in detail of *some of the contradictions which made Russell's Theory of Types* unnecessarily complicated, and made him put in the Axiom of Reducibility. *I went to see Russell a few weeks ago*, and am reading the manuscript of the new stuff he is putting into the Principia. You *are quite right that it is of no importance;* all it really *amounts to is a clever proof of mathematical induction without using the axiom of reducibility.* There are no fundamental changes, identity just as it used to be. *I felt he was too old: he seemed to understand and say "yes" to each separate thing*, but it made no impression so that 3 minutes afterwards *he talked on his old lines. Of all your work he seems now to accept only this: that it is nonsense to put an adjective where a substantive ought to be which helps in his theory of types.*

He indignantly denied ever having said that vagueness is a characteristic of *the physical world.*

He has 2 children now and is very devoted to them. *I liked him very much.* He does not really think *The Meaning of Meaning* important, but he wants to help Ogden by encouraging the sale of it. He wrote a review of it, from which the quotation you saw was taken, in a political weekly.

I had a *long discussion with Moore* the other day, who has *grasped more of your work than I should have expected.*

I'm sorry I'm not getting on better with the foundations of mathematics; I have got several ideas but they are still dim.

I hope you are well, and as happy as you can be under the circumstances. It gives me great pleasure that probably I shall see you soon.

Yours ever
FRANK RAMSEY

After the end of the Lent Term in March 1924 Ramsey went to Vienna. He returned to Cambridge in time for the beginning of the Michaelmas Term to take up a position as lecturer and fellow at King's College. Most of his time in Austria he spent in Vienna, where he was being psychoanalysed. He seems to have associated fairly regularly with Wittgenstein's sister, Mrs. M. Stonborough, and her family circle. Wittgenstein he apparently saw only on four occasions: in March, May and September at Puchberg and in October, just before going back to England, at Otterthal, another village in Lower Austria where Wittgenstein held his last post as schoolteacher.

About the first visit to Puchberg he writes to his mother on 30th March 1924:

I stayed a night at Puchberg last weekend. Wittgenstein seems to me tired, though not ill; but it isn't really any good talking to him about work, he won't listen. If you suggest a question he won't listen to your answer but starts thinking of one for himself. And it is such hard work for him like pushing something too heavy uphill.

And about the visit in May:

I spent last weekend in Puchberg. Wittgenstein seemed more cheerful: he has spent weeks preparing the skeleton of a cat for his children, which he seemed to enjoy. But he is no good for my work.

In the summer Ramsey had a letter from Ogden. Ogden wanted to get the corrections which Wittgenstein had made in the *Tractatus* the year before. Evidently a new edition was contemplated although Ogden also seems to have complained to Ramsey that the book was not selling very well. In his reply to Ogden as of 2nd July Ramsey says:

I shan't see Wittgenstein again till September: can the corrections wait till then? I don't think he will add any more but will be content to endorse the ones we made together last September. The only question is the 4 extra propositions he added in English: whether he would want them printed I don't know. If you want one corrected in September, send me one out, as I want to keep my own. Or if you want one at once I will return it with the corrections I have. He almost certainly wouldn't agree to any more explanatory matter, even Russell's introduction was a strain. I'm sorry so few have sold.

Yours ever

FRANK RAMSEY

To Wittgenstein he wrote:

Mahlerstrasse 7/27
Wien I
15 September 1924

DEAR WITTGENSTEIN,

I wonder if it would be convenient to you if I came to Puchberg to see you next week end ie the 20th. Please say frankly whether you would be bored or pleased to see me. I don't much want to talk about mathematics as I haven't been doing much lately.

I had a letter from Ogden with a large enclosure for you from an American business man, who patronisingly thinks your book not so bad and sends you some stuff of his own, which I will bring or send. There's nothing in it.

Ogden also asked me to get from you, if possible, while I was here any corrections in case there should be a second edition of your book. (This is not really likely.) I have got marked in my copy a lot of corrections we made to the translation, and 4 extra propositions you wrote in English. Obviously I think the corrections to the translation should be made in a new edition, and the only doubt is about the extra propositions; and also you might have something else you would like altered. But it isn't worth while taking much trouble about it yet as a second edition is unlikely. It is merely, I think, that Ogden thought that it might save possible future correspondence for us to talk about it now.

I am here till October 3rd. I don't know if I knew when I last saw you or told you that I have been made a fellow and lecturer in mathematics at King's starting with this coming term.

Yours ever

FRANK RAMSEY

The remaining three communications from Ramsey to Wittgenstein are quite brief. Two are undated and evidently from the time when Wittgenstein was still at Puchberg. The third is dated 22nd October, announcing Ramsey's arrival at Otterthal on the 25th.

After his return to Cambridge in 1929 Wittgenstein resumed contact with Ramsey and had with him the "innumerable conversations" for which he acknowledges his great indebtedness in the Preface to the *Philosophical Investigations*. Ramsey died, at the age of only 26, on 19th January 1930. His premature death, in the words of the editor of his papers, deprived "Cambridge of one of its intellectual glories and contemporary philosophy of one of its profoundest thinkers".

INDEX